Ralph Waldo Emerson

AND TRANSCENDENTALISM

Ralph Waldo Emerson

BARRON'S SIMPLIFIED APPROACH

TO Ralph Waldo Emerson
AND TRANSCENDENTALISM

By Robert L. Gale

ENGLISH DEPARTMENT
UNIVERSITY OF PITTSBURGH

BARRON'S EDUCATIONAL SERIES, INC.

WOODBURY, NEW YORK

TO JOHN

FRONTISPIECE
"Ralph Waldo Emerson" — Culver Pictures, Inc.

CONTENTS

CHRONOLOGY

	Emerson	Other Writers	American History
1803	Born on May 25 in Boston, Massachusetts		Louisiana Purchase, Ohio statehood, South Carolina reinstates slave trade, Supreme Court decision in Marbury vs. Madison establishes right of Court to declare laws unconstitional
1804		Marshall, "Life of George Washington"	Lewis and Clark Expedition (1804-07)
1806		Webster, "Compendious Dictionary"	First Non-Importation Act, Pike's expedition to Colorado
1807		Barlow, "Columbiad"; Irving and Paulding, "Salmagundi" papers (1807-08)	
1808			Importation of slaves forbidden
1809		Irving, "Knickerbocker History of New York"	Non-Intercourse Act bars trade with England and France
1810			West Florida annexed, president empowered to reopen trade with England and France, U.S. population, 7,200,000
1811	Emerson's father dies in May		Charter of Bank of the United States not renewed, Battle of Tippecanoe
1812	Enters Boston Latin School		War of 1812 (1812-15), Louisiana statehood
1813			Battle of Lake Erie, Creek Indian War (1813-14)

	Emerson	Other Writers	American History
1814			British burn White House, Hartford Convention, Lowell cotton mill established
1815		Freneau, "Poems"	Battle of New Orleans
1816			Bank of the United States chartered again, Indiana statehood
1817	Enters Harvard College	Bryant, "Thanatopsis"	U.S.-Canadian border permanently demilitarized, Seminole Indian and Negro uprising in Florida, Mississippi statehood
1818			Seminole uprising quelled by General Andrew Jackson, Cumberland road opened to Wheeling, Illinois statehood, U.S.-British treaty on joint occupation of Oregon territory
1819		Irving, "Sketch Book"	Unitarian Church founded in Massachusetts by W. E. Channing, Alabama statehood
1820	Begins life-long habit of keeping journals	Cooper, "Precaution"	Missouri Compromise (Maine admitted as free state 1820, Missouri as slave state 1821), U.S. population, 9,600,000
1821	Graduates from Harvard in August and soon begins teaching in his brother William's girls' school, Boston	Bryant, "Poems"; Cooper, "The Spy"	Florida annexed
1822		Irving, "Bracebridge Hall"	

	Emerson	Other Writers	American History
1823		Cooper, "The Pioneers" and "The Pilot"	Monroe Doctrine
1824		Irving, "Tales of a Traveller"	Oregon Trail opened as trade route, U.S.-Russian treaty ends dispute over Alaskan border, Owen founds New Harmony, Indiana
1825	Enters Harvard Theological School at Cambridge in February as an irregular student		Erie Canal (1817-25) opened
1826	Licensed to preach as a Unitarian minister in October, leaves for South Carolina and Florida in November for reasons of health (returns to Boston in June, 1827)	Cooper, "The Last of the Mohicans"	Lyceum program begun in Millbury, Massachusetts
1827		Cooper, "The Prairie"; Poe, "Tamerlane and Other Poems"	Irish and German immigrations begin (1827-38)
1828		Cooper, "Red Rover"; Hawthorne, "Fanshawe"; Webster, "American Dictionary of the English Language"	Construction begun on Baltimore and Ohio Railroad, Jackson defeats Adams for presidency, Tariff of Abominations, Workingman's Party formed in Philadelphia
1829	Is ordained at Second Unitarian Church, Boston, in March; marries Ellen Tucker (1811?-1831) on September 30	Irving, "Conquest of Granada"; Poe, "Al Aaraaf, Tamerlane, and Minor Poems"	
1830		Holmes, "Old Ironsides"	Government begins to move Indians to lands west of Mississippi River,

	Emerson	Other Writers	American History
			U.S. population, 12,900 000
1831	Ellen Tucker Emerson dies on February 8	Poe, "Poems"	Nat Turner slave insurrection in Virginia, Garrison founds "The Liberator" (1831-65)
1832	Resigns as Unitarian minister in October, sails for Europe in December	Bryant, "Poems"; Irving, "The Alhambra"	Skirmishes begin between Texans and Mexicans
1833	Visits Italy, France, England, and Scotland, meeting Landor, Wordsworth, Coleridge, and Carlyle; returns to Boston in October	Longfellow, "Outre-Mer"	
1834	Emerson's brother Edward dies in October; Emerson moves to Concord in November	Bancroft, "History of the United States" (1834-76)	
1835	Begins to lecture, in Boston; marries Lydia (Lidian) Jackson (1802-92) on September 14; buys house in Concord	Irving, "Tour of the Prairies"; Longstreet, "Georgia Scenes"; Simms, "The Yemassee"	Second Seminole War (ends 1842); abolitionist tracts burned in Charleston, South Carolina
1836	Emerson's brother Charles dies in May, Emerson publishes "Nature" in September, Transcendental Club is formed in September, Emerson's son Waldo is born in October		Battle of the Alamo (Texas independence recognized 1837)
1837	Delivers "American Scholar" as address in August	Cooper, "Gleanings in Europe" (1837-38); Hawthorne, "Twice-Told Tales"	Michigan statehood, financial panic (followed by depression lasting until 1843), Morse invents telegraph
1838	Delivers "Divinity School Address" in July	Cooper, "American Democrat"; Whittier,	Maine-New Brunswick territorial disputes (settled

	Emerson	Other Writers	American History
		"Ballads and Anti-Slavery Poems"	1842), underground rail-road established to transport runaway slaves
1839	Preaches last sermon in January, daughter Ellen is born in February		
1840	Helps establish "Dial" magazine (editing it 1842-44)	Cooper, "The Pathfinder"; Poe, "Tales of the Grotesque and Arabesque"	Whig Party gains in power, U.S. population, 17,000,000
1841	Hires Thoreau as handyman for a year; "Essays, First Series" published in March; daughter Edith is born in November	Cooper, "The Deerslayer"	Brook Farm experiment begins (lasts until 1847)
1842	Waldo Emerson dies on January 27	Longfellow, "Ballads and Other Poems"	
1843		Poe, "Prose Tales"	
1844	Son Edward is born in July; "Essays, Second Series" is published in October	Whittier, "Voices of Freedom"	"Fifty-Four Forty or Fight"
1845		Cooper, "Satanstoe"; Fuller, "Woman in the Nineteenth Century"; Poe, "The Raven and Other Poems" and "Tales"	Florida and Texas statehood
1846	"Poems" are published in December (dated 1847)	Hawthorne, "Mosses from an Old Manse"; Melville, "Typee"	Iowa statehood, Mexican War declared in May, Oregon boundary settled, Howe invents sewing machine
1847	Leaves in October for England and France	Longfellow, "Evangeline"; Melville, "Omoo"; Prescott, "Conquest of Peru"	Mexican War ends in September, first U.S. postage stamps

	Emerson	Other Writers	American History
1848	Returns to Concord in July	Lowell, "Biglow Papers, First Series"	Peace treaty after Mexican War ratified in May, Wisconsin statehood
1849	"Representative Men" is published in December (dated 1850)	Holmes, "Poems"; Melville, "Mardi" and "Redburn"; Parkman, "The California and Oregon Trail"; Thoreau, "A Week on the Concord and Merrimack Rivers" and "Civil Disobedience"	California gold rush begins
1850	First Western lecture tour (including St. Louis and Chicago)	Hawthorne, "The Scarlet Letter"; Melville, "White-Jacket"; Whittier, "Songs of Labor and Other Poems"	Compromise of 1850 (California to be admitted as free state, states to be organized out of other Mexico-ceded territory without restriction as to slavery, fugitive slaves to be returned more efficiently, etc.); U.S. population, 23,300,000
1851	Denounces Webster and the Compromise Act of 1850, in May	Hawthorne, "The House of the Seven Gables"; Melville, "Moby Dick"	
1852		Hawthorne, "The Blithedale Romance"; "The Poetical Works of Oliver Wendell Holmes"; Melville, "Pierre"; Stowe, "Uncle Tom's Cabin"	
1853	Second Western tour to Ohio, St. Louis, and Illinois (ending in January), mother dies in November		Gadsden Purchase
1854		Thoreau, "Walden"	Commodore Perry opens Japan to American trade, Kansas-Nebraska Act

Emerson	**Other Writers**	**American History**
		(permits squatter sovereignty in Kansas and Nebraska, leads to violence in Kansas in 1855 and 1856)
1855 Emerson helps to found Saturday Club in summer, again lectures along Mississippi River in December	Irving, "Life of George Washington" (1855-59); Longfellow, "Hiawatha"; Melville, "Israel Potter"; Whitman, "Leaves of Grass"	
1856 "English Traits" is published in August	Melville, "Piazza Tales" and "Confidence Man"; Stowe, "Dred"; Whitman, "Leaves of Grass" (second edition)	
1857		Dred Scott decision (against Scott; tested constitutionality of Missouri Compromise and opined that Negroes were not American citizens), financial panic
1858	Holmes, "Autocrat of the Breakfast-Table"; Longfellow, "Courtship of Miles Standish"	Lincoln-Douglas Debates, Republican Party gains strength, Minnesota statehood, stagecoach line is opened from St. Louis to West coast
1859 Emerson's brother Bulkeley dies in May		John Brown raids Harper's Ferry, Virginia, in October, and is hanged in December; Oregon statehood; oil struck in Pennsylvania; Colorado gold rush begins
1860 "Conduct of Life" is published in December	Hawthorne, "The Marble Faun"; Holmes, "Professor at the Breakfast-Table";	Lincoln elected president; South Carolina secedes from the Union; Pony Express opens route from

	Emerson	Other Writers	American History
		Whittier, "Home Ballads and Poems"	St. Joseph, Missouri, to Sacramento, California; shoemakers strike in New England; U.S. population, 31,400,000
1861		Holmes, "Elsie Venner"; Whitman, "Leaves of Grass" (third edition)	Jefferson Davis becomes president of Confederate States in February, Civil War begins in April, Battle of Bull Run in July, "Trent" affair in November
1862	Delivers eulogy on Thoreau in May	Howe, "Battle Hymn of the Republic"	Monitor vs. Merrimack in March, Battle of Shiloh in April, New Orleans captured in May, General McClellan fails to capture Richmond in July, Second Battle of Bull Run in August, General Lee invades North in September, Molly Maguires agitate in Pennsylvania
1863	Officially visits West Point in May	Lincoln, "Gettysburg Address"	Emancipation Proclamation effective January 1, Vicksburg campaign March to July, Battle of Gettysburg in July, draft riots in New York in July, Battle of Chickamauga in September, Chattanooga campaign October and November, West Virginia statehood, Montana gold rush begins
1864		Thoreau, "Maine Woods"	General Grant takes command of Union forces in March, Battle of the Wilderness in May and June, Atlanta falls in July, Battle of Mobile Bay in Au-

Emerson	Other Writers	American History
		gust, Savannah falls in December, Nevada statehood, Tweed Ring corruption begins (lasts until 1871)
1865	Thoreau, "Cape Cod"; Twain, "Celebrated Jumping Frog of Calaveras County"; Whitman, "Drum Taps"	Lee surrenders to Grant in April, Lincoln assassinated in April, harsh reconstruction policy adopted, Thirteenth Amendment abolishes slavery
1866	Whittier, "Snow-Bound"	Atlantic cable completed
1867 "May-day and Other Pieces" are published in April	De Forest, "Miss Ravenel's Conversion"; Lanier, "Tiger-Lilies"; Lowell, "Biglow Papers, Second Series"; Whitman, "Leaves of Grass" (fourth edition); Whittier, "The Tent on the Beach"	Alaska purchased, South divided into military districts, Grange founded, national Ku Klux Klan organized, Nebraska statehood
1868	Alcott, "Little Women"	Fourteenth Amendment grants Negroes citizenship, Susan B. Anthony founds suffragette movement, carpetbagging begins in South, President Johnson impeached and acquitted
1869	Twain, "Innocents Abroad"	Fisk and Gould fail to corner gold, Union Pacific Railroad completed
1870 "Society and Solitude" is published in March	Aldrich, "Story of a Bad Boy"; Harte, "Luck of Roaring Camp and Other Sketches"	Fifteenth Amendment gives Negroes the right to vote, U.S. population, 39,800,000

	Emerson	Other Writers	American History
1871	Visits California in April and May	Eggleston, "Hoosier Schoolmaster"; Hay, "Pike County Ballads"; Whitman, "Leaves of Grass" (fifth edition) and "Democratic Vistas"	Chicago fire, Tammany Ring exposed, Barnum opens circus
1872	Emerson's house burns in July, Emerson leaves in October for Europe and Egypt	Holmes, "Poet at the Breakfast-Table"; Howells, "Their Wedding Journey"; Twain, "Roughing It"	Crédit Mobilier scandal revealed
1873	Returns to Concord in May	Howells, "A Chance Acquaintance"; Twain and Warner, "The Gilded Age"	Financial panic (depression until 1879), Tweed imprisoned, Nevada silver rush begins, gold standard is established
1874		Eggleston, "The Circuit Rider"	
1875	Emerson discontinues regular journal entries, "Letters and Social Aims" are published in December	Howells, "A Foregone Conclusion"; James, "A Passionate Pilgrim and Other Tales"	Black Hills gold rush begins
1876	"Selected Poems" are published in November	James, "Roderick Hudson"; Melville, "Clarel"; Twain, "Tom Sawyer"; Whitman, "Leaves of Grass" (sixth edition)	Bell patents telephone, General Custer and his men annihilated at Little Big Horn, Montana
1877		Adams, "Life of Albert Gallatin"; James, "The American"; Jewett, "Deephaven"	Reconstruction ends, railroad and coal industries strike, Socialist Labor Party organized; Molly Maguire leaders executed
1878		James, "French Poets and Novelists" and "Daisy Miller"; Lanier, "The Marshes of Glynn"	Edison patents phonograph

	Emerson	Other Writers	American History
1879		Cable, "Old Creole Days," Howells, "Lady of the Aroostook"; James, "Hawthorne"	Standard Oil trust formed, Edison patents incandescent bulb
1880		Adams, "Democracy"; Cable, "The Grandissimes"; Howells, "The Undiscovered Country"; Twain, "A Tramp Abroad"	Treaty with China to restrict immigration; U.S. population, 50,200,000
1881		Howells, "A Modern Instance"; James, "Washington Square" and "Portrait of a Lady"	Federation of Organized Trades and Labor Unions founded
1882	Dies on April 27 in Concord	Twain, "The Prince and the Pauper"; Whitman, "Leaves of Grass" (seventh edition) and "Specimen Days and Collect"	
1883	"Writings of Emerson" (1883-87); "Correspondence of Carlyle and Emerson," 2 vols. (1883, 1886)		
1884	"Lectures and Biographical Sketches," "The Senses and the Soul"		
1893	"Natural History of the Intellect and Other Papers"		
1896	"Two Unpublished Essays"		
1903	"Tantalus," "Complete Works of Emerson," 12 vols. (1903-04)		
1909	"Journals of Emerson," 10 vols. (1909-14)		

	Emerson	American History	Other Writers
1912	"Uncollected Writings: Essays, Addresses, Poems, Reviews and Letters by Emerson"		
1933	"Uncollected Letters by Emerson"		
1938	"Young Emerson Speaks: Unpublished Discourses on Many Subjects"		
1939	"Letters of Emerson," 6 vols.		
1959	"Early Lectures of Emerson," 1959 on		
1960	"Journals and Miscellaneous Notebooks of Emerson," 1960 on		
1964	"Emerson-Carlyle Correspondence"		

I. EMERSON'S LIFE

Ralph Waldo Emerson (1803-1882) was the fourth child of William and Ruth Haskins Emerson. Before his marriage in 1796, the father had been an unhappy rural school-teacher and then an only slightly happier rural preacher in the village of Harvard, Massachusetts, a few miles west of his native Concord. Three years after his marriage, he was delighted to accept an invitation to become the pastor of the First Church of Boston. He pleased his congregation with a mild brand of Calvinism which gradually drifted into Unitarianism; in addition, he found time to be something of an intellectual force in Boston as an editor, an occasional writer, and a historian.

A native of Boston, Emerson's mother Ruth was happy to return. There she presented her husband with his first son, John, born in 1799 (died of tuberculosis in 1807); but the following year their first-born child, a daughter named Phebe (1798-1800), died of dysentery when less than two years old. Next they had a second son, William (1801-1868), destined to live longer than any of the eventually eight children except the next to arrive, who was Ralph Waldo, born on May 25, 1803, in Boston.

Emerson was named Ralph after his mother's brother Ralph Haskins, who in 1803 was in the merchant service on the wide Pacific. The name Waldo came from Rebecca Waldo Emerson, one of Emerson's seventeenth-century American forebears, and also from one of his uncles. Emerson regularly called himself and was called Waldo.

Never robust, the Rev. Mr. Emerson became mortally sick early in 1811. He suffered from hemorrhage-weakened lungs and an ulcerated stomach tumor. The decent man remained calm enough concerning his spiritual destination but was worried about his family if they should be left destitute. By this time young Ralph had three more brothers: Edward Bliss (1805-1834), who went insane in his early twenties; Robert Bulkeley (1807-1859), who was always mentally retarded; and Charles Chauncy (1808-1836). In addition there was an infant sister, Mary Caroline (1811-1814), who was only three months old when the father died in May, at the age of forty-two.

Ready, willing, and able to help the bereft mother was Mary Moody Emerson, young Ralph's tough-fibered, no-nonsense maiden aunt who soon began to spend much of her time with her sister-in-law and the children. Emerson's mother was reluctant to ask help of her father, a privateer turned distiller who had in all sixteen children and was soon to die in his eighties. Fortunately the First Church, Boston, voted to pay their minister's widow $500 per year for seven years and allow her temporary use of the parish house, in which she kept most of her family together and in addition took in a few boarders. In this way she supported herself much of her life. Meanwhile young Emerson followed sporadic and desultory day schooling by admittance about 1812 to the celebrated Boston Public Latin School. It was run by a tipsy flogger named William Biglow until he was replaced by Benjamin Gould, a splendidly qualified master. The War of 1812, though it dragged on for a couple of years and stirred up the port city of Boston, did not interfere with Emerson's parsing of Virgil and indeed shook a little doggerel verse out of the perseverant scholar. Few saw signs of future greatness in him, however, and it was his older brother William, first to go on to nearby Harvard

College, on whom the mother, if not shrewder Aunt Mary, pinned most of her hopes.

Ruth Emerson and her family enjoyed a brief sojourn with her mother-in-law and that woman's second minister husband Ezra Ripley, out at Concord in a home later called the Old Manse. Then they returned to Boston in 1815, this time to a succession of other people's homes, usually converted into boarding houses with Emerson's mother as cook and manager. Emerson returned to his studies at the Latin School, starting Greek and improving his facility in English composition and in declamation, and was fortunately permitted to take French lessons on the side. Though not so flashy as his younger brother Edward, now also at the Latin School, Emerson was quietly preparing himself by steady reading and writing for his chance at Harvard, to which he was admitted on a scholarship in 1817.

Harvard College at this time was small and almost pastoral compared to what it became under the reforming hand of President Josiah Quincy a dozen years later. Rules were strict, and young Emerson got to see some of the administration of them through being President John Kirkland's messenger boy. He performed his chores and did his lessons faithfully, but he thought little of his professors, who struck him as mere drillmasters, ordering lines to be memorized one day and delivered the next. Later he must have had their type in mind when he wrote in his lecture "Education" that "A rule is so easy that it does not need a man to apply it; an automaton, a machine, can be made to keep a school so." More enjoyable, therefore, for the shy, tall young fellow was the sense of camaraderie with his noisy schoolmates, for whom he occasionally wrote epigrammatic verse. Best of all was his leisure time, spent in quietly delving into unassigned reading, suggested by chance from many quarters.

What could Emerson look back on when he graduated from Harvard in 1821? Perhaps more than anything else, he would remember the iron band of poverty and the rewards of self-reliance. He existed at Harvard because of church money and the charity of family friends, and because he worked during various vacations teaching school, once during his first collegiate winter when he was only fourteen. He also made a little money writing Boylston prize essays. When he was an upper-classman, the Emerson family felt the pinch a little less because by then his brother William's school for girls, in Boston, had opened and was doing well. Emerson did not become a member of any of the fashionable social organizations, for example the Porcellian and the Hasty Pudding, partly because of his limited finances but mainly because he was naturally a non-joiner. He did associate with a small religious circle and also with a group of serious lads who discussed various philosophical and artistic topics. When he was as young as fifteen, he self-reliantly decided to spend only a minimum amount of time and effort on class assignments. So he lost possible official honors. He graduated thirtieth in his rowdy 1821 class of fifty-nine students. True, he was named class poet, but only after half a dozen higher-ranking fellows had declined the honor. What Emerson gained was well worth the loss.

He took from his teachers what he wanted, which was in the main hints for future reading, thought, and expression. His dazzling Greek teacher, Edward Everett, momentarily tempted him to strive for a glowing if too ornamental style. The solid modern language professor, George Ticknor, more intelligently turned Emerson toward such modern masterpieces as Montaigne's essays and Pascal's *Pensées*. Levi Frisbie and Levi Hedge presented the Edinburgh school of Scottish ethics, essentially anti-Lockean, in such a way as to urge Emerson along the path to Transcendentalism. And Edward Tyrrel Channing, counteracting Everett's inspiration, taught Emerson and many other budding writers to hold rhetorical enthusiasm in check and instead to write simply and graphically. But one of Emerson's most useful influences during these academic years was his non-academic but astute Aunt Mary, who frequently wrote her nephew letters full of hints and probes and prods. Both directly and indirectly, such letters encouraged his growing self-reliance.

For the next three years, Emerson devoted all of his energies to two pursuits: school-teaching and intellectual self-examination. Little though he liked the idea, late in 1821 he became his older brother William's assistant in the latter's private girls' school in Boston, where he taught gently but well for three years. During the last year he was without his brother's encouragement, since late in 1823 William sailed for Germany, where he vigorously studied modern theological philosophy and unsuccessfully urged Emerson to follow. Soon Edward, their younger and initially more promising brother, put his shoulder to the family wheel and followed his graduation from Harvard—first in his class of 1824—by earning good pay as a boys'-school teacher in Roxbury, where the family now lived closer to nature.

School-teaching took time but was not otherwise very taxing. So Emerson had ample energy for a rigorous program of personal reading, in church and literary history, travel works, and belletristic writings. His first published composition, "Thoughts on the Religion of the Middle Ages," appeared in the *Christian Disciple,* November and December, 1822, and reflected his growing temptation to go on in divinity work. Examining himself with merciless honesty, he found a young man with optimism tempered by considerable theoretical awareness of evil and misery, with mounting self-reliance, and with an incipient theory of compensation; further, he found in himself a genuine intuitive moral sense, a talent for eloquence, and also faint but deep little doubts as to the advisability of a religious vocation. Nonetheless, in February of 1825 he entered Harvard Theological School.

For the next four years Emerson vacillated, tacking this way and that but in the long view making substantial professional progress in spite of formidable odds against him. He had not attended divinity school long before his eyes began troubling him so badly that he discontinued reciting in some classes while still attending them. So the next fall and winter he again taught school, this time for a group of boys in Chelmsford, north of Concord; when the new year of 1826 began, he started teaching again at Roxbury, then in the spring at Cambridge, where his charges included Richard Henry Dana, Jr., and Oliver Wendell Holmes's brother John. By now rheumatism, especially in his hip, added to Emerson's misery; and in the fall the afflicted young man, suspecting tuberculosis, took a prolonged vacation, beginning in November, in Charleston, South Carolina, and then St. Augustine, Florida, returning by way of Baltimore, Washington, and Philadelphia the following spring.

Two of his brothers were also a tragic worry. Home from Germany in the fall of 1825, William found it impossible to take Johann Wolfgang von Goethe's personally offered advice and preach what the people wanted to hear rather than what he felt in his heart. So he abandoned the ministry for law and soon moved to New York City to study, supporting himself by translating and teaching. Brilliant Edward distinguished himself as a capable young school-teacher but soon so overtaxed his mind by also studying law under Daniel Webster that in 1828 he had a mental breakdown, from which he never fully recovered.

Still Emerson could point to some progress. In Boston in October, 1826, he preached his first sermon, on the need for unceasing prayer. He almost unceasingly repeated this sermon during his vacation in the South. The following summer, back at Harvard and in better health, he resumed his studies and incidentally picked up his M.A. upon payment of a fee. Then in December he preached most effectively in Concord, New Hampshire, and on Christmas Day, memorably, he first saw Ellen Tucker, later his wife. The following fall and winter, his attendance at Harvard was more regular. In March, 1829, Emerson was ordained at Boston's Second Unitarian Church, where Increase and Cotton Mather had served as ministers.

By this time he was in love with Miss Tucker, quietly to all outward appearances but more intensely than he himself realized. He had visited Concord, New Hampshire, a few times, and the two now looked forward to marriage. With a salary from the Second Church of $100 per month—soon to be increased—all should be well financially. But one worry was the frail health of Ellen, who was evidently an utterly charming, lithe, poetic young lady but who was being inexorably weakened by tuberculosis. Another worry, slight as yet but destined to grow, was the heterodoxy of the honest young minister. He quickly sermonized to his congregation that he preferred moral conduct to expertness in dogma and would never be their moral watchdog; in addition, his absolute sincerity sometimes made him fumble for words during prayer, while his introspective nature occasionally gave him a poor sick-bed and funeral manner.

Emerson and his young wife had little time together. They were married in September, 1829, were beatifically happy, took a few short trips together, and early in 1830 went down to New York and Philadelphia. Ellen wrote a little poetry, as fragile and sentimentally inspiring as she was herself. During their second winter together, she became desperately sick and before spring could come died at the pathetic age of nineteen. Emerson was stoically happy that her suffering had ended, canonized her in his heart as a permanent ideal of goodness and beauty, and regarded his constant sense of her spiritual nearness as a fresh proof of immortality. However, only a few days after her death he wrote in his journal that "There is one birth, and one baptism, and one first love, and the affections cannot keep their youth any more than men."

Ellen's death was a domestic crisis for Emerson. Next came his spiritual crisis. For some time he had had his doubts concerning aspects of Unitarianism and indeed much of the formalism of Christianity in general. He asked his German-trained brother William to summarize all the modern European arguments against supernatural Christianity for him. He began to point out to his young parishioners certain erroneous passages in the Bible or at least difficulties for those who would interpret them. He entertained grave misgivings about the entire ministerial vocation. And as these pressures increased, he began more and more to stress self-reliance and compensation in his journals, and to consider the possibility of an entirely new career—in literature and philosophy. Such modern writers as Thomas Carlyle, Samuel Taylor Coleridge, William Wordsworth, and Goethe began to mean more to him.

Within a year after Ellen's death, Emerson found himself bored by church routine and critical of his dry duties. In July, 1832, the temporary closing of the Second Church for repairs freed him to visit Aunt Mary in Maine and then do a little New Hampshire mountain-climbing. By this time he was sure of his decision. A few weeks earlier he had written a letter to his church officials explaining his specific dissatisfaction with the ordinance of the Lord's Supper. A committee gently enough replied that they could not accept any recommended changes but implied that they wished him to remain. Becoming only the more sure, he prepared a farewell sermon on the subject of communion. Diarrhea intervened, however, to weaken him and therefore delay its delivery until September 9, 1832. Then he simply explained that Christ's last supper was originally only a Passover meal; Christ's language, and that of St. Paul later, should be regarded as figurative; and to convert such language into rigid form was positively anti-Christian. Then resigning at once, he sat back and regrouped his spiritual forces, perhaps hoping that the authorities would allow him to remain on his own terms—they dismissed him instead late in October—but certainly planning to have more to do with literature. To this end he decided to visit Europe.

He wound up his personal affairs. In the summer of 1831 he had begun a suit against the estate of the Tucker family for Ellen's unpaid share. He was happy that his mother, who was still running boarding-houses, was comfortably established in a home on Chardon Street, in Boston. His brother Edward was now sick in Santa Cruz and later Puerto Rico, and was therefore a financial drain even though he was trying to establish a trading business in the West Indies. Charles had been recently admitted to the bar and seemed well on his way to being a fine attorney. William, Edward, and Charles all seemed to understand the spiritual crisis of their brother, but Aunt Mary was appalled by his defection from the church. In any event, armed with little but self-reliant ambition, Emerson set sail from Boston on Christmas Day, 1832, aboard a 236-ton ship bound for Malta.

His decision was exactly right. In Europe Emerson would have the opportunity to see some of the springs of art. He would also converse with a few men whose minds he respected. And he would get away from things American so completely that upon his return his perspective would be wider.

The voyage was uncomfortable, but Emerson after a bit of seasickness soon found himself growing healthier than he had been for years. Two weeks out they saw the Azores; late in January of 1833 they sailed past Gibraltar; and on February 2 the ship docked at Valetta, Malta. Emerson and his four fellow passengers, however, could not do any sightseeing until a two-week period of routine quarantine had transpired. Late in February they took a small ship for Sicily, where they saw the ancient Greek amphitheater at Syracuse and at the end of the month pushed on to Catania to see volcanic Mount Etna and sundry architectural ruins. Next came Messina, Taormina, and then by boat to splendid Palermo, where Emerson drank in the scene and studied Monreale mosaics. The Ides of March bisected his two weeks in glittering Naples, where he paid his respects to Virgil's tomb and much else, including Vesuvius and Pompeii. A jolting coach took him to Rome late in March for three weeks amid its stupendous attractions. He especially responded to Easter Sunday at St. Peter's, the Sistine Chapel, the Vatican statuary, Raphael's "Transfiguration," and Tasso's tomb. Late in April he took a five-day carriage ride to Florence, where he spent a month. He delighted in the Cathedral there, Ghiberti's famous gates, Michelangelo's "David," and that lavish treasury of art the Pitti Palace, which included the "Medici Venus." Perhaps more important even, he met the American sculptor Horatio Greenough and the aging British poet Walter Savage Landor; with the former he discussed functionalism in art, but the latter was curiously disappointing. Late in May he journeyed on to Venice, the dark history of which "oddity" clouded his three days there early in June. After stopping at Milan and dutifully seeking out its imposing Duomo, "The Last Supper" by Da Vinci, and little else, he went on to Switzerland, and so by diligence and steamer to Geneva. He paid his grudging respects to Voltaire's shade at nearby Ferney.

On June 20 Emerson arrived in Paris, taking a room for a full month. He was not sorry. That vibrant city had almost everything he was looking for in Europe: museums bursting with treasures, well-stocked libraries, a provocative natural history exhibit, science lectures honoring the recently dead Baron Cuvier, fine theaters, the opera, and many magnificent buildings. From Boulogne on July 19 Emerson took a steamer for England, the Thames River, and London, which city he strangely pronounced "very dull" but near which, at Highgate, he had a long conversation—or rather audience—with voluble Coleridge on August 5. By mid-August Emerson had toured a little in Scotland, had preached in the Edinburgh Unitarian church, and was heading toward his celebrated meeting with Carlyle, which occurred August 25-26 at Craigenputtock farm near Dumfries. On the 28th, Emerson visited Wordsworth at Mount Rydal, and walked in the garden with the white-haired poet as he recited some of his sonnets. By the end of the month Emerson had been deposited by train at Liverpool, from which port he sailed aboard a 516-ton vessel on September 4 for New York, where he arrived a month later.

The grand tour was over. In Venice Emerson had written in his journal that he was collecting nothing tangible, had nothing in his trunk but old clothes, but that he greatly valued "the growing picture which the ages have painted and which I reverently survey." In Liverpool awaiting passage home, he confided in his journal that he had seen the men he wanted to see: Landor, Coleridge, Wordsworth, and especially Carlyle. Mainly they had shown him by indirections that to learn what he most wanted to know, "that species of moral truth which I call the first philosophy," he must rely only on

himself. But Europe had also helped to make him forever un-
provincial even when he might seem to his critics only a
crotchety Yankee.

In November, 1834, Emerson made a memorable move
—to Concord, Massachusetts. During the previous thirteen
months, he had been restless and almost incoherent in his
movements and his intellectual activities. He supported himself by some little substitute preaching, from Bangor to New
York but mostly in and near Boston. He also began to lecture rather steadily, on a few scientific subjects but more
vigorously on Italy. He turned to a study of the German
language, partly because of Goethe but mostly because of
the example of Carlyle, whose *Sartor Resartus* soon began to
shake many a New Englander. Emerson initiated a magnificent four-decade correspondence with Carlyle by sending his
first letter to Scotland in May of 1834. Emerson roomed for
a short while in the same Boston house with his lawyer
brother Charles. In October the whole family was plunged
into sorrow by the death of Edward, long sick in Puerto
Rico. So when Emerson and his mother settled in Concord,
it was a serious and sober young philosopher who went out
there. But one of his worries—finances—was somewhat di-
minished; according to the executor of the Tucker estate,
Ellen's share would be a little in excess of $10,000 and if
well managed would yield Emerson $100 a month. This would
make it possible for him to survive as he slowly strove to
become a Concord man of letters.

Emerson's journal entry for September 14, 1835, reads:
"I was married to Lydia Jackson." Emerson had met Lidian,
as he later pronounced and spelled her name, in Plymouth,
Massachusetts, her home town, while preaching and lecturing
there the previous year. Through her mother, long dead like
her well-to-do merchant and shipowner father, she was de-

scended from the tough Massachusetts Puritan John Cotton. Unitarian Lidian was well educated but had odd mystical notions for a time, having flirted with Swedenborgianism. Her sister Lucy Brown, married and with two children, had been deserted by her husband; Emerson generously told his wife to use her $600 annual income from her father's dishonestly managed estate to help Lucy. Shortly before his marriage, Emerson bought the recently built Coolidge house in Concord for $3,500, and he and Lidian soon settled there for the remainder of their long lives. They called the place Coolidge Castle and later Bush. With a big house, high taxes, and two maids, they domestically worried about income and expenses. But to Emerson, the eternal verities were always a more legitimate cause for concern.

The year 1836 was a highly significant one for Emerson. It was marked by tragedy, happiness, and intellectual maturing. In little ways he followed the usual ruts of small-town life: he went to the Concord Unitarian church, he served on the local library committee, he worked for a while on the school board, he made room permanently for his mother in Coolidge Castle, and he tried to keep peace between Lidian and volatile Aunt Mary. Lidian gradually shared Aunt Mary's anti-Transcendental notions but not much else with the shrewd, sharp old visitor. An awful tragedy came in May, with the sudden death by tuberculosis of Charles Emerson, whose bereaved brother was stunned by the terrible blow, only the more when a little later, going through his literary effects for possible publishable material, he had to admit that Charles might have been a great speaker but was not much of a writer. The blessed birth in October of the Emersons' first child, Waldo, helped to dispel the clouds of gloom over the house.

Help of a different sort came in several other ways, as

Emerson began to reach out intellectually and exert what at last became an incalculable influence. Kindred Transcendental minds and other admirers sought him out: Bronson Alcott (the father of Louisa May), the Peabody sisters (one of them later married Nathaniel Hawthorne and another married Horace Mann), George Ripley, and many more. Early in September, Emerson published a seminal little book, *Nature,* which was at once either loved or loathed by its many startled readers. Then later the same month, Emerson, meeting with a few others in Ripley's Boston home, founded the Transcendental Club, for the purpose of scholarly discussions on various topics touching upon religion. Finally Emerson rather daringly became his own lecture manager and in December launched a series of twelve papers on "The Philosophy of History." The previous winter he had lectured in Boston on the tamer subject of British literature and had earned over $400, in part by judiciously re-reading the lectures elsewhere. So he was justified in hoping that his second and more characteristic series would also pay.

Next came 1837 and 1838, two years of solidification and then professional crisis. The most notable event was Emerson's delivery of the August 1837 Phi Beta Kappa oration at Harvard; this supremely important speech, "The American Scholar," offended the conservative members of the crowded audience and inspired the ecstatic young. The following July, accepting the innocent invitation of the small graduating class at the Divinity School, Emerson returned to Harvard and stirred up a hornets' nest with his controversial "Address." For insisting on the humanity of Christ, he was branded an infidel, a pantheist, an atheist, and—in the bargain—an obscurantist who was trying to out-Carlyle Carlyle. Anti-Transcendental conservatives in and out of Cambridge joined ranks to attack Emerson from pulpit, class lectern, and study desk. Aunt Mary thought he had gone crazy and had sold out to Satan. Lidian remained loyal and was inspired by her husband's attitude if puzzled by some of his thoughts. Emerson went serenely about his business, which was to study, think, write, and lecture.

Lesser events of these years included continuingly profitable winter lecturing, which netted $500 or $600 for each ten-week season, new and varied friendships with more admirers—for example, James Russell Lowell, Horace Mann, Henry David Thoreau, Jones Very, and Samuel Gray Ward—serenity in the face of national financial panics which threatened the annuities on his invested $22,000 but never ruffled his equanimity, liberal political pronouncements, and, not least, a baby daughter whom Lidian generously insisted on naming Ellen after Emerson's first wife. In a letter to Carlyle, Emerson described the arrival as "a blessed babe, . . . a little fair soft lump of contented humanity, incessantly sleeping, & with an air of incurious security, that says, she has come to stay, has come to be loved . . ."

Next Emerson responded to the appeal of several of his Transcendental friends to edit their newly planned magazine, the *Dial,* by refusing but then giving his moral support to the appointed editor, Margaret Fuller. In July, 1840, the first issue finally appeared, and included Emerson's fine autobiographical poem "The Problem," verse by his friend Thoreau (soon to be a handyman and "pensioner" in Emerson's home for a while), a few bits from the late Charles Emerson's fragmentary journal, and a little poem by the late Edward Emerson. Editing the *Dial* on into early 1842, Miss Fuller then became tired of it, at which time Emerson reluctantly assumed the responsibility until the insolvent journal died with the issue of April, 1844.

While the *Dial* was languishing, Emerson issued his first

volume of essays, in March, 1841. For the most part, the individual essays had grown out of lectures, in some cases from long before; but usually the essays were better developed and more highly polished, if still imperfectly unified. Of the dozen essays in this splendid book, the most significant are "Self-Reliance," "Compensation," and "The Over-Soul," although at first "Love" and "Friendship" were most favorably received. Emerson made next to nothing financially out of his first big book. Carlyle saw to a British printing, complete with his own preface, all of which helped gain Emerson some British converts if no British gold.

So he again went on the lecture circuit. A year earlier he had gone down to New York with a packet of papers to read; while there he stayed briefly with his brother William, then living on Staten Island. In March, 1842, after preparing a fresh supply of lectures and trying them out on winter audiences in Boston, he returned to New York. He did not do well financially, which was most unfortunate since by this time some of the banks in which Ellen's legacy was invested were beginning to default on their payments of dividends. In New York, Emerson met William Cullen Bryant (whose turn from poetry to journalism Emerson always deplored), Horace Greeley, Henry James, Sr., and Albert Brisbane (who was an American popularizer of Fourierism). The rather Fourieristic, communal Brook Farm experiment, started by Ripley and a few others in 1841 at West Roxbury, just outside Boston, never earned much more than the aloof curiosity and reserved sympathy of Emerson, who from the first regarded it as "arithmetic and comfort" and before it was halfway through its seven-year history branded the majority of people who stayed there—including Hawthorne briefly— as adventurers exploiting their few unselfish colleagues. The short-lived 1843 Fruitlands experiment of Alcott attracted

Emerson just as little. Earlier in the same year, again deprived of bank dividends—this time almost a thousand dollars—Emerson wrote up several talks on New England and presented them during a two-month swing through Baltimore, Philadelphia, and New York.

Always homesick when he was on the lyceum circuit, Emerson was happy to return to Concord, even though death had slashed his family yet again. His little son Waldo, only five, had been abruptly cut down by scarlatina late in January, 1842. Emerson wrote in his journal: ". . . this boy, in whose remembrance I have both slept and awaked so oft, decorated for me the morning star, the evening cloud. . . . Every tramper that ever tramped is abroad, but the little feet are still. He gave up his little innocent breath like a bird. Sorrow makes us all children again,—destroys all differences of intellect. The wisest knows nothing." But later, toward the end of his poem "Threnody," occasioned by little Waldo's death, he could honestly write:

> Past utterance, and past belief,
> And past the blasphemy of grief
> The mysteries of Nature's heart . . .

He went on to suggest that Nature by means of death "Pours finite into infinite."

In 1844 two events occurred which are of great importance in American literary history. In September Emerson bought some fourteen acres of land by the shores of Walden Pond, less than two miles south of Concord. The following March his friend Thoreau began clearing a two-acre field on the property and soon started to build his shack, now immortalized in his book *Walden*. The other big event of 1844 was the October publication of Emerson's *Essays, Second Series*. Of its nine essays, all of which are somewhat more down-to-earth than those of the first series, the most important are "The Poet," "New England Reformers," and the violent "Experience."

No one would ever replace dead Waldo in his grieving father's eyes, but a new son, Edward, was born in July, 1844, for compensation nonetheless. The Emerson family of two daughters, Ellen and Edith (born in 1841), and one son was now complete.

For the next couple of years Emerson did not do much that was new. He continued to help Thoreau, Alcott, and Lidian's abandoned sister Lucy Brown; he reluctantly took to the lecture circuit in the winter of 1845-1846; and he became increasingly involved with the abolitionists and therefore was almost as disgusted as Thoreau by the advent of the Mexican War. Then very late in 1846, gathering together his many scattered poems, he published them in Boston in December, with an 1847 date. The most notable poems in the book are "The Sphinx" (which was the tactless opener), "Each and All," "The Problem," "Hamatreya" (which reads oddly for those who know of their author's delight in acquiring farm land), "The Rhodora," "The Humble-Bee," "Woodnotes," "Ode Inscribed to W. H. Channing," "Give All to Love" (of which Lidian probably preferred the beginning), "Merlin," "Bacchus," and finally "Concord Hymn" (the best in the eyes of most contemporary purchasers of the little volume).

The early reviews of Emerson's first book of poems were usually unfavorable. All of the obscure Transcendental philosophy was there. Its awkward Yankee acridity was neither sweetened nor smoothed for the taste and ear of the 1840's. As in his preaching and his written prose, Emerson was ahead of the times with poetry which seemed neither clear nor musical.

But his fame was growing in Europe. Carlyle and others were singing his praises in London and Scotland, and several persons in France had been seeing to his reputation there. So Emerson answered invitations to lecture in England and France, and, installing Thoreau in his home as handyman and guardian, sailed from Boston early in October, 1847, for his second visit to the Old World.

Emerson had the time of his intellectual life in England. He arrived at Liverpool late in October and quickly went to London to see Carlyle and his affable wife. Very early in November he returned to Liverpool and began a series of lectures there and at Manchester. In December he followed a killing pace of lecturing in more than a dozen scattered British towns. Incurring many debts of hospitality, he generously—and in the American spirit—gave a little banquet late in January, 1848, in his Manchester rooms for ten or twelve assorted guests. In February he launched a campaign into redoubtable and somewhat anti-Transcendental Scotland, lecturing in Edinburgh and Glasgow, once in the latter city to an audience which he estimated to be between two and three thousand people. Emerson had the pleasure of conversing with old Thomas DeQuincey in Edinburgh. Next he swung through some provincial Scottish cities, and, stopping in the Lake Country to chat again with aged Wordsworth, returned happily to London for a couple of months. He made intellectual contact with a staggering number of important people: Matthew Arnold, Lady Byron, Arthur Hugh Clough, Richard Cobden, Charles Dickens, Mary Anne Evans (later George Eliot), James Anthony Froude, Sir Charles Lyell, Thomas Babington Macaulay, Richard Monckton Milnes (later Lord Houghton), Lord Palmerston, Coventry Patmore, Alfred Lord Tennyson, and William Makepeace Thackeray were only the beginning.

He remembered the glitter and variety of Paris from his previous visit; so he returned early in May but was somewhat disappointed. There was a poetic justice in his now preferring London, which in 1833 he had naively called dull. But in Paris he visited the Louvre, attended the theater, sampled some street rioting, heard Alphonse de Lamartine at the French Assembly, and consorted mostly with English-speaking persons until his happy return to London after a little less than a month.

Evidently his money was running so short that he decided to read some more papers, usually old ones, at two or three halls; his total earnings, about £125, helped but were less than he had hoped for. However, the enthusiasm of his final audiences was genuinely touching, and Emerson said so. Then he and Carlyle took a final little trip together, to Stonehenge and Salisbury. At last Emerson had to return to Liverpool, from which port in mid-July he took a steamer for Boston again, where he arrived on July 27, 1848. On the way home, he must have contrasted his two trips to Europe: in 1833 he had gathered impressions; this time he had gathered crowds.

His advancing age, Lidian's return to conventional religion, a maturing family, happy farming, and investment and lecturing opportunities all contributed in the next several years to make Emerson somewhat less idealistic, more practical, even a trifle materialistic. He became quicker to seize an agricultural or a fiscal chance; at the same time, however, he remained a youthful father to gay children, a restrained champion of progressivism, and essentially what Lowell aptly called him in *A Fable for Critics:*

A Greek head on right Yankee shoulders, whose range
Has Olympus for one pole, for t'other the Exchange;
He seems to my thinking (although I'm afraid
The comparison must, long ere this, have been made),

A Plotinus-Montaigne, where the Egyptian's gold mist
And the Gascon's shrewd wit cheek-by-jowl coexist . . .

In the summer of 1850, having lectured through the two
previous winters only in Rhode Island, New York, Phila-
delphia, and New Jersey, Emerson went on the first of many
Western speaking engagements. Going by way of Buffalo and
Niagara Falls to Cleveland, he pushed on to Cincinnati, the
Mammoth Cave of Kentucky (not lecturing there), down the
Ohio River to Cairo and then up the broad Mississippi River
to St. Louis; then he returned home via Chicago, Lake
Michigan, Niagara again, Lake Ontario, and so to Boston
again. Late the following winter, he read papers on "The
Conduct of Life" in Buffalo and Pittsburgh. He could no
longer use any lectures on representative heroes, since from
the first of January, 1850, his book *Representative Men* was
available. It uncontroversially discussed Plato, Swedenborg,
Montaigne, Shakespeare, Napoleon, and Goethe.

Emerson in May of 1851 violently attacked Daniel Webster's support of the Compromise of 1850. Once an adored
hero, Webster was now shamed in Emerson's eyes. After
Webster's famous "Seventh of March Speech," Emerson wrote
in his journal that "The word *liberty* in the mouth of Mr.
Webster sounds like the word love in the mouth of a courtezan." Of the Fugitive Slave Law, which the odious Compromise included, Emerson wrote, "This filthy enactment
was made in the nineteenth century, by people who could
read and write. I will not obey it, by God." In his May speech
at Concord, Emerson publicly enunciated his loathing of
Webster, suggested that all Negro slaves be purchased and
freed even if it cost thousands of millions of dollars, and as
for the Union, why talk of it when such a gulf divided North
and South?

In the winter of 1852-1853 Emerson was off again to the

wild West, lecturing first in Cincinnati and then just after Christmas in St. Louis. In January he began to conquer Illinois, reading papers in Springfield and Jacksonville; after returning to St. Louis to double back for Cleveland via the Mississippi River and then the Ohio, he reported back home again with a thousand dollars and innumerable impressions for profit. In 1854 he lectured in Detroit, Chicago, and Milwaukee; and late in 1855 he penetrated as far west as eastern Iowa, beyond the Mississippi, which by then was a familiar friend.

Several events occurred which interlocked with his lecture tours in the 1850's. In July of 1850, Margaret Fuller, returning from Italy with her Italian husband Angelo Ossoli and their child, drowned with them during a storm off Fire Island. Early in 1852 Emerson, with two other persons, published a two-volume book called *Memoirs of Margaret Fuller Ossoli* and including some sensible critical commentary. In November of the following year Emerson's mother, aged eighty-four, died after contentedly living with her son and Lidian for almost two decades. In August, 1854, Emerson's whilom disciple and part-time handyman Thoreau published his matchless *Walden,* and it thrilled his mentor to see his own love of nature and his philosophy of self-reliance so magnificently expressed by a kindred spirit. Then in July, 1855, a practically unknown Brooklynite named Walt Whitman sent Emerson a copy of his *Leaves of Grass.* Within a few days Emerson had absorbed its essential messages of democracy, freedom, and pantheism, and on July 21 wrote its author to commend his "extraordinary" verse and to greet him "at the beginning of a great career." Once again, Emerson was an uncanny prophet.

In the four years immediately preceding the Civil War, Emerson strangely mellowed and prospered, while at the same time he turned himself into a red-eyed abolitionist. A mere summary of his intermittent lecturing, which covered roughly the same old terrain even as he earned higher and higher pay, is wearying; so Emerson, who did the endless traveling, must have been Spartan indeed. In January, 1856, he lectured in bitterly cold Illinois and then returned by way of Ohio. A year later he read papers in Philadelphia, and then Rochester, Chicago, and Cincinnati. In December of the same year he followed successes in New York and Philadelphia by going into Canada with his speeches. In the spring of 1858 he lectured in Boston and Philadelphia. Then in January and February, 1860, he again invaded the Middlewest, reading lectures in Detroit, Chicago, and Wisconsin, often under primitive conditions. Still he felt that it was worth it in more ways than financial. In 1858 he earned nearly $2,000 on the circuit, and always he was learning more and more about his varied country.

In the same period, Emerson published two books—*English Traits,* 1856, and *The Conduct of Life,* 1860—both of which had grown out of his lectures. Within a month of publication, *English Traits* was in its second printing and was receiving deservedly fine reviews. Even Carlyle, increasingly distressed by Emerson's philosophical airiness, praised the book highly. Published on the eve of the Civil War, *The Conduct of Life* was also popular with the public and the critics alike, including Carlyle; but the work now seems less lustrous, for two reasons: its philosophy is more practical than Transcendental, and at the same time it ignored the coming holocaust of civil war.

In 1855 Emerson helped to found the famous Saturday Club, a social group whose membership was strictly limited to the most cultured men in Boston. At first the Saturday Club included, in addition to Emerson, only Louis Agassiz,

Richard Henry Dana, Jr., John Sullivan Dwight, Rockwood
Hoar, James Russell Lowell, John Lothrop Motley, Benjamin
Peirce, Samuel Gray Ward, Edwin Percy Whipple, and
Horatio Woodman. Later the Club admitted Nathaniel Haw-
thorne, Oliver Wendell Holmes, William Dean Howells,
Henry James, Sr., Henry Wadsworth Longfellow, Charles
Eliot Norton, Francis Parkman, William Hickling Prescott,
Charles Sumner, and John Greenleaf Whittier, among others
less noteworthy. After Emerson's death, Holmes celebrated
the illustrious group in a charmingly sentimental little poem
called "At the Saturday Club," from which the following lines
concern Emerson:

> From his mild throng of worshippers released,
> Our Concord Delphi sends its chosen priest,
> Prophet or poet, mystic, sage, or seer,
> By every title always welcome here.
> Why that ethereal spirit's frame describe?
> You know the race-marks of the Brahmin tribe,—
> The spare, slight form, the sloping shoulder's droop,
> The calm, scholastic mien, the clerkly stoop,
> The lines of thought the sharpened features wear,
> Carved by the edge of keen New England air.

This Club helped establish the *Atlantic Monthly,* in 1857;
Lowell, its first editor, was a member, and most of his con-
tributors were fellow-members. A more relaxing development
was the Adirondack Club, a hiking and camping group which
the Saturday Club members organized for summer vacations.

In the spring of 1859 Emerson's mentally retarded brother
Bulkeley died at the age of fifty-two. That winter Captain
John Brown, the fanatic hero of Bloody Kansas, lectured at
the Concord Town Hall and then quietly slipped away to
become the controversial martyr of Harper's Ferry. A few

weeks before his execution on December 2, Emerson, who knew him rather well, bravely referred to Brown in a Boston lecture as a saint.

The Civil War did not much alter Emerson's habit of going on winter lecture tours. In January, 1862, he spoke at the Smithsonian Institution in Washington, and soon thereafter, through Senator Sumner and Secretary of State William Henry Seward, met President Abraham Lincoln, whom he slowly began to respect highly. In the winter of 1862-1863 Emerson went west, to Chicago and Milwaukee, and also Indianapolis, Pittsburgh, and Montreal. The following December he spoke in· various parts of New England on America's future, and in the process turned savagely on England for its pro-Southern stand. During the last winter of the War he again lectured in New England, repeating his consistent position that it was more important to win the war and end slavery that it was to preserve the Union; in January, 1865, he again carried his message to Chicago and Milwaukee.

During the war, death thinned the ranks of civilians about Emerson. In May, 1862, Thoreau died, and Emerson read an eloquent eulogy of the magnificent philosopher-naturalist. In May, 1863, crotchety old Aunt Mary, almost ninety and long since established with a Long Island niece, died and was returned to Concord for burial. And in May, 1864, unidealistic but intriguing Hawthorne died without ever really coming to an understanding with Emerson, who thought that solitude had killed the novelist before he ever thoroughly showed his greatness in his writings. Death might have claimed Emerson's son Edward too if the young man had had his way. Slight and sickly, he took an arduous five-month trip to Omaha, Fort Laramie, Salt Lake City, Sacramento, San Francisco, and Panama, hoping to build up his health and then join the Union army, to his father's unphilosophical con-

sternation. But Edward failed in his endeavor and returned
unhappily to Harvard. Later he studied medicine abroad and
at Harvard, and became a physician.

Emerson had a semi-official if minor part in the war on
three occasions. He responded to the Emancipation Procla-
mation, effective January 1, 1863, by writing his splendid
"Boston Hymn," which includes these lines:

> To-day unbind the captive,
> So only are ye unbound . . .

That May, Emerson served on a board of visitors inspecting
West Point; his excited observation of artillery exercises gave
him an un-Transcendental respect for gunpowder. Finally,
in April, 1865, he lifted up his voice in tremendous praise of
the martyred Lincoln, the humor-loving, kind, sensible, poetic, wise leader.

It is an exaggeration, but not a thoughtless one, to say
that Emerson was also a casualty of the Civil War. In the
"Channing Ode" he had written,

> If I refuse
> My study for their politique,
> Which at the best is trick,
> The angry Muse
> Puts confusion in my brain.

But the war inevitably dragged him from his study and the
"honied thought" hived there. Some confusion resulted. Emerson unphilosophically praised the violence of war. He spoke
of lifting sword and rifle himself; yet he could not face the
prospect of his son's joining up. At first he did not see the
wisdom of Lincoln's policy of Union above all and felt instead
that "amputation is better than cancer." It is possible that

some of Emerson's war-time utterances gave moral support to the sort of irrational anti-Southern sentiment which, after Lincoln's death, made possible the miseries of Reconstruction days.

From the end of the Civil War until his house partly burned in July, 1872, the story of Emerson's life is one of gradual decline in spite of some outward appearances to the contrary. It is true that in December, 1865, he lectured in New York, and then in January and February swung resolutely out west again as far as Wisconsin and Iowa. A year later he conducted a routine but profitable course of lectures in Boston. In January, 1867, he went back west, this time to Minneapolis, St. Louis, and Kansas; December of the same year found him in Chicago and Des Moines. He repeated some papers in Boston the following fall and, a little later in Providence. Early in 1870 he made the mistake of agreeing to present a series of sixteen formal lectures at Harvard on philosophy; the work proved irksome and unprofitable. In the spring of 1871 he agreed to revise and repeat his Harvard lectures; he—and his students—were relieved when an invitation to go to beckoning California permitted him gracefully to cut his course short. Through all of these laborious lectures, Emerson was steadily weakening.

Arrived at by easy stages including a private Pullman car part of the way, California was a thrilling and restful interlude in the too-busy life of the aging philosopher for part of April and May, 1871; but November of the same year found him in Chicago and elsewhere in the chilly Middlewest, and a few weeks later down in Baltimore and Washington. In April, 1872, Emerson repeated his latest type of platform performance, conversational reading of poetry with commentary. At this time his memory, which for a few years had been growing slightly weaker, began to decline dangerously. His audiences formerly had been inspired or irritated; now they became mostly sympathetic.

Time had been bringing Emerson more proofs of mutability. His wife Lidian no longer was sympathetic with his non-Christian Transcendentalism and went back to straight Unitarianism. In 1865 his younger daughter, Edith, married a fine ex-cavalry officer named Will Forbes and thereafter naturally went partly out of her father's shrinking life. In 1867 one of his closest non-intellectual friends, Abel Adams, died; long a financial adviser, this good man had paid the way of Emerson's son Edward through college, and in his will he left the Emerson family $5,000. The next year Emerson's brother William, who had retired in Concord after a long career as a Wall Street lawyer, died, leaving Emerson the lone survivor of the family.

The beginning of the slow end was an event tersely recorded as follows in Emerson's journal for July 24, 1872: "House burned." With their children all away, Emerson and Lidian fought the fire themselves until help could come, carried out manuscripts and books and clothes, and got wet, cold, and frightened. Within a little while Emerson was sick and feverish. But his innumerable friends must have cheered him, and their generosity was astonishing. The insurance was almost sufficient to pay for all necessary repairs, but on top of that friends sent more than $17,000, while more pledges and offers were being gratefully declined. Noticing that Emerson looked very sick, his son-in-law Forbes got him out of a nagging obligation to prepare a volume of essays for some British publishers who had been troubling him for a couple of years. The work was later put together for the aging Emerson by his daughter Ellen and his literary aide and later executor

James Elliot Cabot, and became *Letters and Social Aims,* published in 1875.

Emerson's other works, issued after the war, were popular but mild, and included his second book of poems, *May-day and Other Pieces,* 1867, and *Solitude and Society,* 1870. The ornaments of *May-day* are "Brahma," "Boston Hymn," "Days," and the mercilessly honest "Terminus." *Solitude and Society* includes "Civilization," "Farming," and "Works and Days." In addition, Emerson provided the introduction in 1870 for an American edition of Plutarch's *Morals* and in 1874 compiled an anthology called *Parnassus* containing his favorite poems—with nothing by Edgar Allan Poe, Walt Whitman, or himself.

Emerson and his devoted daughter Ellen left in 1872 for Egypt. Their entire seven-month journey involved Emerson in a variety of experiences which were destined to be the final momentous ones in his long life. From New York they took a steamer late in October, docked at Liverpool less than two weeks later, and quickly went to London and to Thomas Carlyle. By mid-November they were in Paris, attended by James Russell Lowell, Henry James, Jr., and a traveling servant whom they engaged for the coming trip. Lyons, Marseilles, Nice, Genoa, Leghorn, and Pisa led late in the month to Florence, and shortly after that Rome for a couple of weeks. Then Emerson and his daughter went to Naples and boarded a steamer there for Alexandria, where they arrived on Christmas Day.

By January 7, 1873, they had gone to Cairo, rested there, and begun a leisurely Nile River excursion, which took them to Thebes, Luxor, Idfu, and as far south as Aswan. One of their companions from a sociable riverboat nearby was Teddy Roosevelt, then fourteen years of age and accompanied by numerous older Roosevelts. Mid-February found Emerson and Ellen back in Cairo, greatly refreshed and enlightened by all that they had seen, and soon they were steaming via the Straits of Messina back to Naples. In Rome they were helped by James again; then after a few more days in Florence they arrived back in mid-March in Paris, where Emerson met Ernst Renan, Hippolyte Taine, and Ivan Turgenev. When April arrived in England, so did the Emersons, for the start of a bewildering social whirl: Robert Browning, Carlyle, George Eliot, William Gladstone, Froude, and John Stuart Mill were not all—simply the most gifted—of the brilliant people who paid their respects to Emerson, who with his daughter soon went on to Oxford, meeting John Ruskin among others there, then elsewhere in England and so to Scotland. Finally, they went back to Liverpool and on May 15 departed for Boston and home.

Emerson's last nine years were mostly effortless. Bush, his home at Concord, was restored by insurance money and the generosity of friends and now became his haven. Lidian was an ever more sociable, amiable, and admirable companion. Their daughter Ellen was his secretary and guardian; in the last few years, she organized a group of Concord friends, whom she called the bodyguard, to watch out for her father if he should absent-mindedly wander and require help in getting home. Gradually near-senility settled easily upon him but was never complete. Stories of his asking where he was going to lecture, what topic he was about to read a paper on, who was in the open coffin at Longfellow's funeral, and where Thoreau might be may all be balanced against clear proof of sudden flashes of lucidity even shortly before his death. He continued to lecture, often far afield, longer than he should have; but Ellen usually accompanied him and the audiences were almost always aware that they were in the presence of a saintly soul and the remnants of a titanic mind.

One of the most amusing occurrences toward the end was on the occasion of Mark Twain's supposedly humorous speech at Whittier's birthday banquet in 1877. Twain leveled his wild Western satire at three members of the Boston literati —Longfellow, Holmes, and Emerson. All were present, but Emerson could not understand Twain's words or their import; so the funnyman's remorseful apology which he later sent was unneeded. Perhaps the saddest occurrence was Emerson's bemused reading of some of his own ringing essays from the past and remarking to his daughter, "Why, these things are really very good."

Indeed they were, and so was their author, who, ten days after a long walk in the cold night air, died of pneumonia on April 27, 1882.

II. LETTERS, SERMONS, AND LECTURES

Considerable understanding of Emerson the personality, the thinker, and the literary man can be obtained by a careful reading of his best letters, early sermons, and various lectures.

Letters

Emerson was a prolific letter writer. Before Ralph L. Rusk's monumental edition of the letters, published in six big volumes in 1939, seven major groups of Emerson's letters had been published—those to Thomas Carlyle, Henry David Thoreau, Carlyle's protégé John Sterling, Samuel Gray Ward, Herman Grimm (son and nephew of the Grimm brothers who collected German fairy tales), William Henry Furness (a friend from childhood on), and Arthur Hugh Clough. In his edition Rusk calendared all of these letters, corrected previous erroneous readings and misprintings, and published all other available letters—some 2,000 not printed before. Containing a fine introduction and a superb index of almost three hundred double-columned pages, Rusk's edition is a masterpiece of imaginative and meticulous scholarship. In 1964 a comparably expert edition of the Emerson-Carlyle correspondence, correcting previous editions, was published by Professor Joseph Slater.

To Various People

Although Emerson's letters are of more interest to scholars than to general readers, they form an invaluable part of the Emerson canon. They show his personal, often unguarded responses to a myriad of topics, books, poems, illustrious persons, friends, and acquaintances. Without consulting the letters, one cannot for example know fully what Emerson thought about Louis Agassiz, Delia Bacon, John Brown, Egypt, *Faust*, Annie Fields, Edward Gibbon, Gray's "Elegy," Horatio Greenough, *Hamlet*, Nathaniel Hawthorne, Julia Ward Howe, Iowa, Henry James, the *Journal of Speculative Philosophy*, Emma Lazarus, Abraham Lincoln, music, Negroes, Charles Eliot Norton, Theodore Parker, Rome, Saadi, George Sand, Sir Walter Scott, Emanuel Swedenborg, *Two Years Before the Mast*, Jones Very, *Walden*, Daniel Webster, John Greenleaf Whittier, and a hundred other significant persons, places, and things.

In addition, those who want clarification of a point in Emerson's biography can profitably consult pertinent letters. His depths of tenderness and his stoic strength both appear in a letter to Aunt Mary in February, 1831, on the occasion of his wife Ellen's death: "My angel is gone to heaven this morning & I am alone in the world & strangely happy. Her lungs shall no more be torn nor her head scalded by her blood nor her whole life suffer from the warfare between the force & delicacy of her soul & the weakness of her frame." The thirty or so extant letters which Emerson wrote during his first trip abroad throw light on his moods, activities, and sources of special pleasure and instruction. From Naples in March, 1833, he wrote a friend:

. . . here in Naples I am lonely & a-'cold & my chamber is dark, & who can go to Vesuvius or Paestum or the

Villa of Cicero when the rain pours? However, to be just, when the sun shines, it does seem a decent place, yea, its Chiaia (as they call the range of palaces on the margin of the bay,) its islands, & surrounding mountain country, marvellously beautiful. I crawled out the other day between the drops to Baiae, & since, have been to Pompeii & Herculaneum, & I could not help thinking I was paid for my pains. . . . I am not going to pester you with description of this unrivalled landscape. I leave it to the painters.

The first letter from Emerson to his wife Lidian, in April, 1836, ends neatly with "write me a long letter & love your Waldo E." In May of the same year he wrote majestically of his brother Charles, recently dead: "I can never bring you back my noble friend who was my ornament my wisdom & my pride.—A soul is gone so costly & so rare that few persons were capable of knowing its price and I shall have my sorrow to myself for if I speak of him I shall be thought a fond exaggerator. . . . I feel not only unfastened . . . and adrift but a sort of shame at living at all." Emerson's reports back to Concord during his lecture tours make his movements clear enough; for example, on June 16, 1850, he wrote from St. Louis: "From Russellville, I went on by stage to Hopkinsville, slept there a few hours, thence took the stage for Eddyville, 40 miles; there, after five or six hours, took a steamboat and went down the Cumberland River to Paducah, 72 miles. At Paducah, I took the steamboat Genl Washington (from Louisville) to this place, 220 miles. and arrived here last night about 9 o'clock." Sometimes he has more exciting events to report. In January, 1863, he was caught in a hotel fire at Niagara Falls: ". . . at 3 o'clock, was waked by the cry of Fire! within the house. I put on my clothes or some of them, & gathered up my properties as many & as fast as I could in the dark, & got down stairs through a cloud of smoke & cinders, and found women clothed in blankets & barefooted in the hall & in the street, & great distress everywhere. The house was burned out thoroughly, before all our eyes, & nothing left but the four walls." Almost a decade later, the aging Emerson penned a gay but imperfectly focused description of crowds on the streets of Cairo:

> If you could look into the mob of all colors & costumes & of no costume at all who crowd the streets & lanes of this aged city, you would be sure you were dreaming, & rather more wildly than is pleasant. Turk, Copt, Arab, Nubian, Italian, German, English & American men & women fill the narrow unpaved streets & lanes of this old town with all their own costumes & colors & languages & manners Nothing is so odd as to attract more than a moment's attention where the next moment brings a new wonder and in every corner a new novelty, outdoing the last.

That was almost all he wrote in one day. He evidently started another letter to Lidian in Egypt and concluded it about five months later in England. Inevitably the old hand finally lost its cunning. After 1873 the letters are always short and more and more frequently include misspellings. But as late as 1878—and undoubtedly later—he was still honest with himself. He wrote his daughter Edith at that time as follows: ". . . I ought to have informed you earlier that I am fast losing almost the power of speech even, & therefore necessarily confiding myself to my Study, where I can still read with intelligence." In 1880 there are only seven letters. The longest is two paragraphs and in draft form has several pathetic spelling errors; the shortest is only a one-line thank-you. The last

letter, in July of 1881, sends good wishes to an Emerson society.

It must be admitted that Emerson was not a great letter-
writer, in the sense that Benjamin Franklin, Henry James,
or Theodore Dreiser, for example, were. Too often his Transcendental position made him serious when lightness might
have been more appropriate and seemingly aloof when profound sympathy was needed. Only moderately effective is the
following precocious humor, from a letter in January, 1820,
to his brother Edward: "I am not going to trouble you with
all the long apologies of letterwriters young and old when they
have been negligent for after using a few pages of their epistle
in this excusing & excusable introduction it generally amounts
after all to nothing more or higher than mine,—laziness &
procrastination." On the other hand, Emerson surely enters
insufficiently into the misery of the Hawthornes, following the
death by drowning of the novelist's sister Louisa in July, 1852;
Emerson ends a one-paragraph letter of sympathy as follows:
". . . who knows which is the shortest & most excellent way
out of the calamities of the present world?"

To Thomas Carlyle

The Emerson-Carlyle correspondence is one of the greatest and most important of its sort in the history of literature.
It began in May, 1834, when Emerson, having gestated the
memory of meeting Carlyle nine months before, hesitantly
opened what became a forty-year exchange of letters ultimately totaling more than two hundred. In bulk, half of the
letters were written before the first decade had run its course.
Emerson begins by recording the fact that mere chance ac-
quainted him, before his trip to Europe, with Carlyle's original
and profound writings. ". . . I said: This person has come
under obligations to me & to all whom he has enlightened.

. . . Drawn by strong regard to one of my teachers I went to see his person & as he might say his environment at Craigenputtock." Emerson then praised Carlyle's serially published *Sartor Resartus* and sent copies of Webster's speeches and a friend's Swedenborgian treatise. Carlyle replied some three months later, discussing Teufelsdröckh (as he always called his *Sartor Resartus*), his move to London, his plans for a book on the French Revolution, and his gratitude to Emerson for his kind gifts and kinder words. Carlyle described his sense of Emerson's visit: "Among the figures I can recollect as visiting our Nithsdale Hermitage, . . . there is perhaps not one of a more undoubtedly *supernal* character than yourself: so pure and still, with intent so charitable; and then vanishing too so soon into the azure Inane . . ." In November, 1838, Carlyle's magnificent wife Jane penned a unique postscript to her husband's letter to Emerson which is deeply moving: "'*Forgotten you?*' O no indeed! If there were nothing else to remember you by, I should never forget the Visitor, who years ago in the Desart descend [*sic*] on us, out of the clouds, as it were, and made one day there look like enchantment for us, and left me weeping that it was only *one* day. . . . I read all that you write with an interest which I feel in no other writing but my Husband's . . ." Emerson's second letter, in November, 1834, reports the death of his brother Edward, opens a discussion on Goethe, and expresses hope that the Carlyles may visit America. "Your letter . . . made a bright light in a solitary & saddened place. I had quite recently received the news of the death of a brother, . . . whose loss to me will be a life-long sorrow. As he passes out of sight, come to me visible as well as spiritual tokens of a fraternal friendliness which by its own law, transcends the tedious barriers of Custom & nation, & opens its way to the heart." He preferred the unpopular *Sartor Resartus* to Goethe: "Far far better seems to me the unpopularity of this Philosophical Poem (shall I call it?) than the adulation that followed your eminent friend Goethe. . . . I cannot but regard it as his misfortune with conspicuous bad influence on his genius,—that velvet life he led. . . . Then the Puritan in me accepts no apology for bad morals in such as *he*." But Emerson listened respectfully to Carlyle's friendly epistolary lectures on Goethe; indeed, throughout the correspondence Carlyle as the older and at first professionally more successful man seems to take the intellectual and even stylistic lead. His letters are more fun. Emerson's, however, are always sincere and are in addition illuminating.

It was thirteen years before Emerson saw Carlyle again, in London. During those years their understanding and love for one another were kept alive and grew through their remarkable letters. Emerson expressed his constant hope through the late 1830's that his friend would come with his wife to America, be his guest for a year, and return to London laden with profits from a series of lectures in Boston and elsewhere. The care with which Emerson went into all expenses and probable income clearly shows his Yankee shrewdness to his Scottish correspondent. And it was Emerson who wrote a preface to the first book edition of *Sartor Resartus,* which was published in Boston in 1836. In November of the next year Emerson saw to the American publication of Carlyle's next book, which was quickly in Emerson's hands. He wrote Carlyle:

> Instantly I . . . went straight to Boston, and have made a bargain with a bookseller to print the *French Revolution.* It is to be printed in two volumes of the size of our American *Sartor,* one thousand copies, the estimate making the cost of the book say (in dollars and cents)

$1.18 a copy, and the price $2.50. The bookseller con-
tracts with me to sell the book at a commission of
twenty per cent on that selling price, allowing me however to take at cost as many copies as I can find sub-
scribers for. There is yet, I believe, no other copy in the
country than mine: so I gave him the first volume, and
the printing is begun. . . . I shall sustain with great
glee the new relation of being your banker and attorney.

In February, 1838, Emerson wrote: ". . . I confide in sending
y[ou] seven hundred dollars at least as a certificate that you
have so many readers in the West." A month later Emerson
was making arrangements for an American printing of
Carlyle's *Miscellanies.* An enterprising New York literary
pirate issued Carlyle's *Heroes and Hero Worship* before Emerson could see to its more honorable publication in Boston.
When American cash for the *Miscellanies* actually began to
arrive, Carlyle promised to buy a horse, to be called "Yankee"
and ridden to improve its grateful master's chronic poor health.
    Emerson kept intellectual as well as financial channels
open. He sent Carlyle his little book *Nature,* of which his
friend wrote perceptively:

You say it is the first chapter of something greater. I
call it rather the Foundation and Ground-plan on
which you may build whatsoever of great and true has
been given you to build. It is the true Apocalypse this
when the "open secret" becomes revealed to a man. I
rejoice much in the glad serenity of soul with which you
look out on this wondrous Dwelling-place of yours and
mine,—with an ear for the *"Ewigen Melodien,"* which
pipe in the winds round us and utter themselves forth in
all sounds and sights and things . . . You will see what

the years will bring you. It is not one of your smallest qualities in my mind, that you *can* wait so quietly and let the years do their hest.

Carlyle's response to Emerson's "American Scholar" is even more notable:

> I coul[d have] *wept* to read that speech; the clear high melody of it went tingling thro' my heart; I said to my wife "There, woman!" She read; and returned and charges me to return for answer, "that there had been nothing met with like it since Schiller went silent." My brave Emerson! And all this has been lying silent, quite tranquil in him, these seven years . . . May God grant you strength, for you have a *fearful* work to do! . . . O for God's sake *keep yourself still quiet*. Do not hasten to write; you cannot be too slow about it. Give no ear to any man's praise or censure . . .

In a letter to Carlyle, Emerson called the furor occasioned in Cambridge and Boston by his "Divinity School Address" a "storm in our washbowl." Carlyle was indifferent to the storm: "As to you, my friend, you are even to go on, giving still harder shocks if need be . . ." But best of all in Carlyle's view were Emerson's *Essays,* the first series of which arrived in London in May, 1841:

> The voice of one crying [in] the desart;—it is once more the voice of a *man.* . . . Objections of all kinds I might make, how many objections to superficies and detail, to a dialect of thought and speech as yet imperfect enough, a hundredfold too narrow for the Infinitude, the real vision and belief of one, seen face to face: a "voice of the heart of Nature" is here once more. . . . Persist, persist; you have much to say and to do. . . . You are

a new era, my man, in your new huge country: God give you strength, and speaking and silent faculty, to do such a work as seems possible now for you!

In November, 1844, Carlyle saw to a London edition of these essays and even furnished a brief preface; of the kindnesses, Emerson wrote gratefully and modestly as follows:

> It was thoughtless in me to ask your attention to the book at all in the proof state: the printer might have been fully trusted with corrected printed pages before him. Nor should Chapman [the publisher] have taxed you for an advertisement; only, I doubt not he was glad of a chance to have business with you; and, of course, was too thankful for any *Preface*. . . . A preface from you is a sort of banner or oriflamme, a little too splendid for my occasion, & misleads. . . . If you introduce me, your readers & the literary papers try to read me, & with false expectations. I had rather hav[e] fewer readers & only such as belong to me.

In March, 1847, Carlyle voiced qualified praise for Emerson's poems:

> . . . in spite of my hardheartedness, I did gain tho' under impediments a real satisfaction, and some tone of the Eternal Melodies sounding, afar off, ever and anon, in my ear! . . . A grand view of the Universe, everywhere the sound (unhappily, *far off*, as it were) of a valiant genuine Human Soul: this, even under rhyme, is a satisfaction worth some struggling for. But indeed you are very perverse; and thro' this perplexed *un*-diaphanous element, you do not fall on me like radiant summer rainbows, like floods of sunlight, but with *thin* piercing radiances which affect me like the light of the

> *stars.* It is so: I wish you would become *concrete,* and
> write in prose the straightest way; but under any form
> I must put up with you; that is my lot.

In the years before their 1847 reunion, Emerson wrote
Carlyle about other Americans, sometimes sending copies of
their works and occasionally asking traveling Americans to
call upon Carlyle. Thus, reading Emerson's letters to his con-
frere enables students to understand his opinions on Bronson
Alcott, William Ellery Channing the younger, Margaret
Fuller, F. H. Hedge, Henry James, Sr., Sampson Reed, George
Ripley, Charles Sumner, Henry David Thoreau, Jones Very,
and Daniel Webster, among others. Sometimes Carlyle responded sagely; sometimes less so or not at all. Thus, after
reading an essay by Thoreau, he wrote in May of 1847 about
"A vigorous Mr Thoreau,—who has formed himself a good
deal upon one Emerson, but does not want abundant fire and
stamina of his own . . . In plain prose, I like Mr Thoreau
very well; and hope yet to hear good and better news of him
. . ." Emerson shared the growing pains and death agonies of
the *Dial* magazine with Carlyle, who replied with cogent
criticism on issue after issue. Knowing that Alcott was a
curious fellow, Emerson wisely wrote this in March, 1842, to
alert Carlyle before his personal appearance:

> If you have heard his name before, forget what you
> have heard. Especially if you have ever read anything
> to which this name was attached, be sure to forget that;
> and, inasmuch as in you lies, permit this stranger when
> he arrives at your gate to make a new & primary impres-
> sion. I do not wish to bespeak any courtesies or good or
> bad opinion concerning him. You may love him, or hate
> him, or apathetically pass by him, as your genius shall
> dictate: Only I entreat this, that you do not let him go

quite out of your reach until you are sure you have seen him & know for certain the nature of the man. And so I leave contentedly my pilgrim to his fate.

The greatest sorrow of his life, the death of his son Waldo, Emerson described in poignant words which ended with this gracious link to his friend Carlyle: "How often I have pleased myself that one day I should send to you, this Morningstar of mine, & stay at home so gladly behind such a representative!"

Then the two friends, who had seen each other once and only overnight then, met again in London after fourteen years. Their letters to each other during Emerson's eight-month stay in Europe, mostly in England and Scotland, are necessarily less informative or profound. Then the Atlantic Ocean again separated them from July, 1848, until late in 1872—and very late in their lives—when they met again in London. The quarter-century separation is regularly filled with letters, gradually more widely spaced but containing much evidence of undiminished affection and admiration. In the first heyday of their correspondence, they averaged four or five letters per year apiece. But in the 1850's, each wrote only a time or two a year; in fact, only one short letter seems to be extant for 1857. They continued, of course, to send each other their books, critical comments thereon, and always words of encouragement.

In April, 1866, Carlyle's beloved wife Jane died; Emerson learned the news from a friend and immediately wrote Carlyle a wonderful message of comfort: "The stroke long-threatened has fallen at last, in the mildest form to its victim, & relieved to you by long & repeated reprieves. I must think her fortunate also in this gentle departure, as she had been in her serene & honored career. We would not for ourselves court covetously the descending steps, after we have passed the top of the mount, or grudge to spare some of the days of decay. And you will have the peace of knowing her safe, & no longer a victim." Then, noting that he never saw her physical decline, he reminisced on her youth: ". . . her conversation & faultless manners gave assurance of a good & happy future. . . . I can . . . still recall vividly the youthful wife & her blithe account of her letters & homages from Goethe, & the details she gave of her intended visit to Weimar, & its disappointment." Then, "I could heartily wish to see you for an hour in these lonely days." Strangely enough, the bitterly isolated Carlyle did not reply for eight wretched months.

Emerson did not write again for three years. In the 1870's the old men exchanged a mild little flurry of letters mostly on the subject of bequests and old thoughts and mild work. In June, 1870, Emerson reported a Boston newspaper story that Carlyle was going to visit America: "Make that story true, though it had never a verisimilitude since thirty odd years ago . . ." But Carlyle gloomily shook his head from across the ocean: "The Visit to America, alas, alas, is pure Moonshine. . . . I do sometimes talk dreamily of a long Sea-Voyage, and the good the Sea has often done me,—in times when good was still possible. . . . Thank you a thousand times for that thrice-potential welcome, and flinging wide open of your doors and your hearts to me at Concord. The gleam of it is like sunshine in a subterranean place." Emerson remained more sweetly mellow. He wrote Carlyle in January, 1872, before he saw him again on his way to Egypt. In this final important letter Emerson beautifully thanked Carlyle for a princely gift of his thirty-two-volume Library Edition— "now my stately collection is perfect." Then he expressed his gratitude at having known such a man: "I count it my eminent happiness to have been so nearly your contemporary, and your friend—permitted to detect by its rare light the new star almost before the easterners had seen it, & to have found no disappointment, but joyful confirmation rather, in coming close to its orb."

And in this way Emerson turned the last leaf. The Emerson-Carlyle correspondence is one of the glories of the English-speaking world. Emerson's part in it reveals a man uniformly sincere, considerate and helpful, self-reliant, spiritually alive, and ever hopeful of the best. Emerson reveals all of these traits in many of the hundreds of other letters he wrote to other friends, but he shines most clearly in his letters to Carlyle.

Sermons

Emerson's sermons are important because they help to throw light on his early life and to show the beginnings of his literary style. More important, they also reveal that early in his career he held numerous conventional theological opinions —for example, on the nature of God, on the obligations of charity to those less fortunate, and on miracles. We know from reading his later writings that he grew less conventional —positively radical, some of his contemporaries would say.

On Various Occasions

Quite conventional are these words from Emerson's sermon called "The Christian Minister: Part II" (March 15, 1829): "The account that we give of the existence of the human race is the benevolence of the Deity, who doth not sit in the solitude of his own perfections but rejoices in adding continually and infinitely to the amount of happiness and pouring forth around him the profusion of being and of joy." As for charity, Emerson preached in "Self and Others" (January

12, 1831) as follows: "It might be shown that it is an indispensable part of a finished character to comply with the law of charity. It might be shown that he who withholds his aid from his fellow man is more a loser than his fellow man from whom he withholds it . . ." And in his sermon called "Miracles" (January 23, 1831) he points out that ". . . the only way by which men's attention can be aroused to the thought that there is a presiding Intelligence, is to startle them by a plain departure from the common order, as by causing the blind to see and the dead to arise."

Many of Emerson's later written passages are quite different from the three quotations above from the sermons. In his journal on April 23, 1838, Emerson impatiently wrote this: "Last night the old question of miracles was broached again at the Teachers' Meeting, and shown up and torn up in the usual manners. They think that God causes a miracle to make men stare and then says, Here is truth. They do not and will not perceive that it is to distrust the deity of truth—its invincible beauty—to do God a high dishonor,—so to depict him." And in his essay "Self-Reliance" we find an equally unconventional passage on charity: "Then again, do not tell me, as a good man did to-day, of my obligation to put all poor men in good situations. Are they *my* poor? I tell thee, thou foolish philanthropist, that I grudge the dollar, the dime, the cent I give to such men as do not belong to me and to whom I do not belong. . . . alms to sots . . ."

Changed in some respects though Emerson became from the early sermon-writer, he remained theologically consistent in many important ways. From the start he placed the highest value on the individual's reason and moral conscience. In an early sermon on "Forgiveness" (April 5, 1829) he preached as follows: "I wish your credit and consideration to this doctrine no whit farther than it forces itself on your own conviction." From that comment to his famous statement in "Self-Reliance" is but a step: "No law can be sacred to me but that of my nature." Moreover, from the start Emerson always inveighed against a foolish adulation of the past. Thus, in his first sermon, "Pray Without Ceasing" (October 15, 1826), he liberally advised: "Be not deceived; for what is the past? It is nothing worth. Its value, except as means of wisdom, is, in the nature of things actually nothing." This sounds very much like many of his provocative utterances in "The American Scholar," including among others the following: "The book, the college, the school of art, the institution of any kind, stop with some past utterance of genius. This is good, say they,— let us hold by this. They pin me down. They look backward and not forward." In other respects too, Emerson's early sermons lead naturally into his later essays and poems.

The best way to gain a notion of Emerson the Unitarian preacher is to read *Young Emerson Speaks: Unpublished Discourses on Many Subjects*, edited by Arthur Cushman McGiffert, Jr., in 1938. This well-edited collection of twenty-five sermons excellently shows both the continuity and the evolution of Emerson's theological and moral thinking. It has a useful introduction, thorough notes, a list of the 171 extant sermons with dates, and a helpful index. Because Emerson's sermon "The Lord's Supper" is readily available, McGiffert does not print it. This famous sermon, which was Emerson's farewell to the Unitarian congregation of the Second Church, Boston, reveals that by October, 1832, when it was delivered, Emerson had changed into a radical but tolerant free-thinker.

The Lord's Supper

"The Lord's Supper" starts with a bang. Its text is this: "The kingdom of God is not meat and drink; but righteousness, and peace and joy in the Holy Ghost" (Romans 14:17).

Emerson begins by showing that over the centuries the communion of the Last Supper has caused controversy. He goes on logically: "Having recently given particular attention to this subject, I was led to the conclusion that Jesus did not intend to establish an institution for perpetual observance when he ate the Passover with his disciples; and further, to the opinion that it is not expedient to celebrate it as we do." The main body of the crisply ordered sermon follows. First Emerson weighs all the evidence from the Gospels, showing that he is completely conversant with them. Then he concludes ". . . first, that it does not appear, from a careful examination of the account of the Last Supper in the Evangelists, that it was designed by Jesus to be perpetual; second, that it does not appear that the opinion of St. Paul, all things considered, ought to alter our opinion derived from the Evangelists." Next Emerson considers the implications of the intellectual position which says in effect that, while granting that the ceremony was not designed to be perpetual, it is traditional, widespread, and beneficial. The trouble is that communicants in the rite point incorrectly to Christ as the authority for it, and that they also vacillate between worship of God and of Christ. Worse, a combination of bread and wine is foreign to us. And finally, exalting and adhering to a mere form, "after it is outgrown, is unreasonable, and it is alien to the spirit of Christ." Emerson concludes personally by saying that since his congregation intends to retain the rite, which he cannot conscientiously administer, he must resign.

It is my desire, in the office of a Christian minister, to do nothing which I cannot do with my whole heart. Having said this, I have said all. I have no hostility to this institution; I am only stating my want of sympathy with it. Neither should I ever have obtruded this opinion upon other people, had I not been called by my office to administer it. That is the end of my opposition, that I am not interested in it. I am content that it stands to the end of the world, if it please men and please Heaven, and I shall rejoice in all the good it produces.

Lectures

In General

Emerson's hundreds of lectures, insofar as they can be assembled or reconstructed, are now in process of editing and publication. The project is obviously a big one. Many of the lectures turned into published essays. In addition, some of the lectures are available in the twelve-volume Centenary Edition of Emerson, published in 1903-1904. In 1932 Professor Clarence F. Gohdes published summaries of seven Emerson lectures as reconstructed from newspaper accounts. In a 1946 *New England Quarterly* article, Miss Jeanne Kronman edited three more lectures. But the only comprehensive edition, now under way, is *The Early Lectures of Ralph Waldo Emerson,* edited by Professor Robert E. Spiller and the late Stephen E. Whicher. The first volume, appearing in 1959 and covering the years 1833-1836, includes lectures on science, the inner lives of great men (Michelangelo, Milton, and Burke, among others), and English literature (for example, the writings of Chaucer, Shakespeare, and Bacon). As Spiller and Whicher aptly remark concerning Emerson in their introduction, "The three sources of inspiration for his ideal American scholar were now complete: nature (science), books (literature), and action (the lives of great men)."

A popular and once often reprinted lecture was "Historical Discourse at Concord," which Emerson delivered at the second centennial anniversary of the town of Concord, on September 12, 1835. This was a tactful gesture on the part of Emerson, who was still considered a newcomer by old Concordians. So he spent a couple of months doing hard research into local history. The resulting lecture praised the original settlers, summarized the natural lore, and paid respect to the hospitality of the now ruined redskin, indicated the origins and progress of local self-government, and summarized Concord's part in the Revolution. Emerson gracefully closed by expressing "unwillingness to quit the remembrance of the past" and by identifying himself with Concord—"Humble as is our village in the circle of later and prouder towns that whiten the land, it has been consecrated by the presence and activity of the purest men."

Without a doubt, the two most important lectures Emerson ever delivered are "The American Scholar" and "Divinity School Address." Most of Emerson's great essays, for example "Self-Reliance" and "Compensation," derived from lectures; but "The American Scholar" and "Divinity School Address" were strictly lectures, each written for a specific occasion and not revised for later essay publication.

The American Scholar

"The American Scholar," delivered on August 31, 1837, to the Phi Beta Kappa Society, Harvard College, is Emerson's most popular lecture; more than that, it is one of the most influential pieces of writing in the history of American literature. It is logical, practical, and inspiring. It may be divided into four main parts: a brief introduction, in which Emerson greets his audience startlingly and then criticizes the degradation of specialization; then the heart of the lecture, a consideration of the three main influences upon the true scholar; next a summary of a scholar's duties; and finally a brief indication of hopeful signs in America now.

Emerson seems to begin courteously—"Mr. President and Gentlemen: I greet you on the recommencement of our literary year." But instantly he becomes startling and critical: "Our anniversary is one of hope, and, perhaps, not enough of labor. . . . Thus far, our holiday has been simply a friendly sign of the survival of the love of letters amongst a people too busy to give to letters any more." He then valuably adds that by specializing "Man is . . . metamorphosed into a thing, into many things. . . . The priest becomes a form; the attorney a statute-book; the mechanic a machine; the sailor a rope of the ship." Even the scholar is demeaned into a specialist; in his proper state, he should be *"Man Thinking."*

The three influences on the scholar are nature, the past, and the world of action. Probably because Emerson published his little book *Nature* in 1836 and did not wish to repeat himself, he keeps brief his discussion of the influence of nature on the scholar. The scholar sees in the wondrous spectacle of beginningless, endless nature a resemblance to his own infinite spirit. "He shall see that nature is the opposite of the soul, answering to it part for part." Youth sees the individual and diverse aspects of nature; but the perceptive observer sees interconnections throughout, "and remote things cohere and flower out from one stem." Whole sciences, for example, astronomy and geometry, become related. Finally it is revealed that knowing oneself and studying nature are two aspects of one thoughtful endeavor.

Perhaps the most unusual part of "The American Scholar" now follows. The past is valuable, says Emerson, only as it quickens the present into thought. We can study the past in many ways, through art or institutions, for example; but the most efficient means is through books. "Books are the best of things, well-used; abused, among the worst. What is the right use? What is the one end which all means go to effect? They are for nothing but to inspire. I had better never see a book than to be warped by its attraction clean out of my own orbit, and made a satellite instead of a system." Far from idolizing great books, we should realize that "Cicero, Locke, and Bacon [for example] were only young men in libraries when they wrote these books." Apply to the present what those past authors wrote, and remember that "Each age . . . must write its own books; or rather, each generation for the next succeeding. The books of an older period will not fit this." Since nature and action also inspire man thinking, he should never forget that "Books are for the scholar's idle times."

Next Emerson turns to the realm of action. "Action is with the scholar subordinate, but it is essential. Without it he is not yet man. Without it thought can never ripen into truth." We must give the lie to the foolish notion that scholars should be impractical old hermits. The true thinker is always ready to venture forth heroically and measure his theories beside reality. More than this, he should be anxious to have his thinking disturbed by noisy action. "I do not see how any [thoughtful] man can afford, for the sake of his nerves and his nap, to spare any action in which he can partake. It is pearls and rubies to his discourse. Drudgery, calamity, exasperation, want, are instructors in eloquence and wisdom. The true scholar grudges every opportunity of action past by, as a loss of power. It is the raw material out of which the intellect moulds her splendid products." It is also true, however, that the dust of action must settle so that the contours of thought can emerge and be seen. What the scholar experiences is really a rhythm, a counterpoint: "The mind now thinks, now acts, and each fit reproduces the other. When . . . thoughts are no longer apprehended and books are a weariness,—he has always the recourse *to live*."

Finally, Emerson treats scholarly duties and reasons for optimism in America in the 1830's. The scholar is obliged to cut through appearances to factual reality. He is to expect no great honors to fall upon him, in fact "must relinquish display and immediate fame." Also "he must accept—how often! —poverty and solitude," knowing that his work is by its very nature inefficient. But he can comfort himself by realizing that he is "exercising the highest functions of human nature," and is "preserving and communicating heroic sentiments, noble biographies, melodious verse, and the conclusions of history." Above all, he must be confident and self-trusting. Looking about him for hopeful signs, Emerson next points out that "Instead of the sublime and beautiful, the near, the low, the common" are now being studied and turned into art. In contrast to the "cold and pedantic" Pope, Johnson, and Gibbon, more recent writers such as Burns, Goethe, Wordsworth, and Carlyle are "blood-warm." Emerson's last thought, which was misunderstood by conservative auditors to be cheap Yankee jingoism, is instead an impassioned plea for down-to-earth native individualism: "We have listened too long to the courtly muses of Europe. . . . We will walk on our own feet; we will work with our own hands; we will speak our own minds. . . . A nation of men will for the first time exist, because each believes himself inspired by the Divine Soul which also inspires all men."

Divinity School Address

Delivered on July 15, 1838, to the senior class in the Divinity College, Cambridge, "Divinity School Address" repeats the argument that the essence of the past must be alive now if the past is to mean anything in the present. But Emerson applies his daring anti-traditional attack specifically to formalized Christianity. Thus the lecture relates to his farewell sermon "The Lord's Supper" in criticizing dry forms, and it relates to his "American Scholar" lecture in espousing personal intuition and experience. "The American Scholar" called for independent intellectual endeavor; "Divinity School Address" calls for untrammeled spiritual activity.

Emerson begins his "Address" by describing the "refulgent" beauty of nature *now,* and suggests that its message is that those whose intuitive response to it is moral are divine: "If a man is at heart just, then in so far is he God . . ." Then he points out pantheistically that God is everywhere: ". . . the world is not the product of manifold power, but of one will, of one mind; and that one mind is everywhere active, in each ray of the star, in each wavelet of the pool . . ." He goes on characteristically: "Good is positive. Evil is merely privative, not absolute: it is like cold, which is the privation of heat." The perception of this omnipresent, divine goodness is the source of religion. To this intuitive, universal perception Jesus Christ made—and makes—a unique appeal. Now comes the unusual follow-up. This truth cannot be indoctrinated. "It cannot be received at second hand. Truly speaking, it is not instruction, but provocation, that I can receive from another soul. What he announces, I must find true in me, or reject; and on his word . . . I can accept nothing." It follows that ministers are wrong when they insist that "Miracles, prophecy, poetry, the ideal life, the holy life, exist as ancient history merely . . ." The fountains of ancient inspiration are flowing today. Each person must go to them himself.

Christ's priceless message, that "God incarnates himself in man" and that "man's life was a miracle, and all that man doth [is]," His followers have distorted, so that now "churches are not built on his principles, but on his tropes. Christianity became a Mythus . . ." Next Emerson attacks historical Christianity for two failings. First, he says that, like all who attempt to communicate religion, Christian churchmen have exaggerated the importance of ritual. "All who hear me, feel that the language that describes Christ . . . is not the style of friendship and enthusiasm to a good and noble heart, but is appropriated and formal . . ." But the best religion is one "which shows God in me . . ." Truly religious poets do this: "They admonish me that the gleams which flash across my mind are not mine, but God's . . ." And second, Emerson rebukes traditional Christian leaders because "the Moral Nature . . . is not explored [by them] as the fountain of the established teaching in society. Men have come to speak of the revelation as somewhat [i.e., something] long ago given and done, as if God were dead." The sad result of formalizing Christianity and making it merely historical is "the universal decay and now almost death of faith in society." Instead of showing "the moral sentiment in application to the duties of life," modern ministers ruin the Sabbath: "it is unlovely; we are glad when it is over." Some sermons are so lifeless that the imaginative listener must day-dream to keep from being offended. The typical preacher avoids revealing any part of his own life. One minister to whom Emerson once listened "had no one word intimating that he had laughed or wept, was married or in love, had been commended, or cheated, or chagrined. If he had ever lived and acted, we were none the wiser for it." One reason that sermons are mere "thoughtless clamor" is that "tradition characterizes the preaching of this country; . . . it comes out of the memory, and not out of the soul." Emerson's inevitable conclusion is that "historical Christianity destroys the power of preaching, by withdrawing it from the exploration of the moral nature of man."

Sensibly, Emerson asks what the remedy is for the young minister. Worship individual man. Be yourself and imitate no one, not even the best, because "Imitation cannot go above the model." As for your parishioners, "be to them a divine man; be to them thought and virtue; let their timid aspirations find in you a friend; let their trampled instincts be genially tempted out in your atmosphere; let their doubts know that you have doubted, and their wonder feel that you have wondered." Do not seek the applause of society. Use adversity as a militant challenge to rise. Above all, use the two advantages which Christianity has given us: "the Sabbath, the jubilee of the whole world"; and the right to preach. And when you preach, show "the world to be the mirror of the soul."

Thoreau

Emerson's obituary address (revised before publication) of his friend Henry David Thoreau, who died in May of 1862, is both moving and informative. As such, it has a high place among his public speeches. Emerson begins by briefly tracing Thoreau's ancestry and early indifference to any "craft or profession." He then points out Thoreau's various talents, precious virtues, and renunciations (Emerson makes Thoreau out to be more of a stoic than he was). Thoreau found it easier to say no than to say yes. He loved children. He went to jail for refusing to pay his town tax. He intimidated book-guarding librarians with the ferocious argument that the only proper custodian of books was the person who needed them. Thoreau loved the simplicity of Indians and the newness of America more than the sophistication and decay of Europe. He was an aloof individualist, a true and patient nature-lover (whom nature loved in return), and a Transcendentalist in that his "excellent wisdom . . . showed him the material world as a means and symbol." Emerson is a little critical when he points out Thoreau's "whim which grew on him by indulgence, yet appeared in gravest statement, namely, of extolling his own town and neighborhood as the most favored center . . ." Emerson is critical of his friend's poetry: "His own verses are often rude and defective. The gold does not yet run pure, is drossy and crude. The thyme and marjoram are not yet honey. But if he want lyric fineness and technical merits, if he have not the poetic temperament, he never lacks the causal thought, showing that his genius was better than his talent." Next Emerson overemphasizes Thoreau's "disappointments," as expressed in *Walden* in the riddle of the hound, the bay horse, and the turtledove. Then, in a famous rebuke, Emerson inveighs against his friend's indifference to intellectual ambition. "I so much regret the loss of his rare powers of action, that I cannot help counting it a fault in him that he had no ambition. Wanting this, instead of engineering for all America, he was the captain of a huckleberry-party. Pounding beans is good to the end of pounding empires one of these days; but if, at the end of years, it is still only beans!" Finally Emerson closes by generously quoting from his noble friend's journals and by shrewdly noting what was exactly right: "The country knows not yet, or in the least part, how great a son it has lost."

Education

The stimulating lecture "Education" Emerson prepared late in life. It was not published until after his death, in *Lectures and Biographical Sketches,* 1884. It is notable for its stress on the individualism of each student, Emerson's automatic distrust of educational institutions when they set themselves over the individual and deny his unique requirements, the need to consider physical and vocational education and manual training, and Emerson's hearty optimism and practical liberalism. It is also marked by an admirable directness and simplicity of style.

Emerson begins by dramatically praising our free educational system: "the poor man, whom the law does not allow to take an ear of corn when starving, nor a pair of shoes for his freezing feet, is allowed to put his hand into the pocket of the rich, and say, You shall educate me, not as you will, but as I will . . ." Then Emerson insists on the unitary nature of education. Far from being something which goes on only in school, it is a process which takes place in nature, in the household, in business, in the world of action. As we learn, we classify and gain power over nature. (All of this relates to "Nature," "The American Scholar," and "Experience.") Aspects of every tedious day offer to teach us something (note Emerson's poem "Days").

Then Emerson espouses pragmatism when he writes as follows: "the event of each moment, the shower, the steamboat disaster, the passing of a beautiful face, the apoplexy of our neighbor, are all tests to try our theory, the approximate result we call truth, and reveal its defects." Next he deplores the fact that just as our culture in aiming to train the mind ignores the spirit, so it also ignores the body, eye, and hand. Thus education is woefully incomplete. "The great objects of Education should be commensurate with the object of life. It should be a moral one; to teach self-trust: to inspire the youthful man with an interest in himself; with a curiosity touching his own nature; to acquaint him with the resources of his mind, and to teach him that there is all his strength, and to inflame him with a piety towards the Grand Mind in which he lives." (All of this relates to "Self-Reliance" and "The Over-Soul.")

Letting his theory inspire him, Emerson becomes practical and offers concrete suggestions. First off, he advises parents not to insist that their children follow vocationally in their footsteps. "A low self-love in the parent desires that his child should repeat his character and fortune, an expectation which the child, if justice is done him, will nobly disappoint. . . . Cannot we let people be themselves, and enjoy life in their own way? You are trying to make another *you*. One's enough." Do not downgrade apparently ordinary children too hastily. They are like flies in their ability to get in anywhere and "see the inside of the show. . . . They are there only for fun, and not knowing that they are at school, in the court-house, or the cattle-show, quite as much and more than they were, an hour ago, in the arithmetic class." And children judge us with uncanny accuracy. "They know truth from counterfeit as quick as the chemist does. They detect weakness in your eye and behavior a week before you open your mouth. . . . If I can pass with them [Emerson sagely adds], I can manage well enough with their fathers." And solitude teaches the "obscure youth" during his "quiet search."

Now Emerson offers some suggestions for the classroom teacher. "Respect the child," he says three or four times; "stop off his uproar, fooling and horseplay—keep his nature and arm it with knowledge in the very direction in which it points." Encourage his hobbies, which can be exceptionally educative. While you keep up his enthusiasm, require much drill, because "Accuracy is essential to beauty." For this reason, "It is better to teach the child arithmetic and Latin grammar than rhetoric or moral philosophy, because they require exactitude of performance . . ." Do not encourage your charges to correct you; but if you make a mistake, and the pupil "sets you right, hug him [or her]!" The relationship of teacher to pupil should resemble that of mother and child. "The child is as hot to learn as the mother is to impart," and the taught child then has "a fury to impart" to another what he has just learned.

Next comes severe criticism of large, democratically managed classes and their inevitably lowered standards. Emerson plainly states that not everyone can or deserves to be formally educated. Some youths "are more sensual than intellectual. Appetite and indolence they have, but no enthusiasm. These come in numbers to the college: few geniuses: and the teaching comes to be arranged for these many, and not for those few. . . . You have to work for large classes instead of individuals; you must lower your flag and reef your sails to wait for the dull sailors; you grow departmental, routinary, military almost with your discipline and college police. But what doth such a school to form a great and heroic character?" (This was a good question in 1880, and it is an even better one today.)

A good teacher needs patience, as much patience as "the naturalist [who] learns all the secrets of the forest, of plants, of birds, of beasts, of reptiles, of fishes, of the rivers and the sea . . ." With sufficient patience, a teacher may conclude of even the "rogue and dunce" in school, who "requires a cruel share of time," that "If he has his own vice, he has its correlative virtue. Every mind should be allowed to make its own statement in action, and its balance will appear." Emerson even has a prophetic word about teaching machines: "A rule is so easy that it does not need a man to apply it; an automaton, a machine, can be made to keep a school so. It facilitates labor and thought so much that there is always the temptation in large schools to omit the endless task of meeting the wants of each single mind, and to govern by steam [or, now, electronics]. But it is at frightful cost. Our modes of Education aim to expedite, to save labor; to do for masses what cannot be done for masses, what must be done reverently, one by one . . ."

Having been both idealistic and practical, Emerson concludes with comprehensive optimism. "Talk of Columbus and Newton! I tell you the child just born in yonder hovel is the beginning of a revolution as great as theirs." It is up to the teacher—and parent, and every adult—to encourage that "revolution" and teach by example. "Have the self-command you wish to inspire. . . . Teach them to hold their tongues by holding your own. Say little; do not snarl; do not chide; but govern by the eye. See what they need, and that the right thing is done." The teacher should combine the virtues of male and female—"The will, the male power" and "Sympathy, the female force." The teacher is permitted to be funny once in a while. "I advise teachers to cherish mother-wit. . . . smuggle in a little contraband wit, fancy, imagination, thought." Finally, realize that "By simple living, by an illimitable soul, you inspire, you correct, you instruct, you raise, you embellish all. By your own act you teach the beholder how to do the practicable."

Emerson was a tireless correspondent, a persuasive preacher, and a forceful and original lecturer. His letters, sermons, and lectures repay the most careful study. They are always sincere and provocative. However, to understand the essential Emerson, one must go to the heart of the man, his *Journals,* and then to his most characteristic literary works—his essays and his poems.

III. JOURNALS

Whoever hopes to approach an understanding of Emerson must give a great deal of attention to his *Journals*. These voluminous diaries and notebooks were published only in part by Emerson's son Edward Waldo Emerson and Emerson's grandson Waldo Emerson Forbes, in ten volumes, 1909-1914. This edition gives a slightly idealized picture of Emerson. It omits much material, usually passages in which Emerson expresses skepticism, horror at many unpleasant aspects of life, and his own mild earthiness. To save space, this edition also omits material which found its way into published essays, sometimes in quite different form. On the whole, the first edition of Emerson's *Journals* is excellent and still highly useful. A fine one-volume abridgment of it was prepared by Bliss Perry as *The Heart of Emerson's Journals* in 1926 (now available in a Dover paperback), and it became something of a best-seller in the curious Roaring Twenties. In 1960 Robert N. Linscott prepared an excellent Modern Library abridgment of the *Journals*.

Now well under way is a complete edition of the 182 journals (E. W. Emerson and W. E. Forbes used only ninety-four) kept by Emerson for more than half a century—from 1819 until 1875. It is called *The Journals and Miscellaneous Notebooks of Ralph Waldo Emerson*. Publication started in 1960 under the general editorship of Professor William Gilman; the whole edition will eventually come to sixteen volumes or so.

Perhaps the best way to begin a study of this complex mass of material is with Perry's 350-page edition, *The Heart of Emerson's Journals.* The selections are representative, the various headnotes are to the point and useful, and the index is helpful.

Emerson writes on almost everything under the sun in his *Journals,* but in general the entries fall under four main headings: friends, authors and their works, significant events, and what we might call great ideas. Reading through this edition of the *Journals* from beginning to end, one comes away with incredible respect for the mind of Emerson, who for fifty mature years thought, read, talked, and responded to his intellectual and social and political and natural world with infinite curiosity and absolute honesty. In no sense an autobiography, the *Journals* nonetheless provide materials for Emerson's spiritual and intellectual biography.

The sage of Concord knew almost everyone of importance in the United States, certainly in New England. He freshly recorded his personal impressions about presidents, statesmen, artists, authors, visiting dignitaries, and so on. When he was near Washington in 1827, Emerson saw President John Quincy Adams: "Mr. Adams went out a swimming the other day into the Potomac, and went near to a boat which was coming down the river. Some rude blackguards were in it, who, not knowing the character of the swimmer, amused themselves with laughing at his bald head as it poppled up and down in the water, and, as they drew nearer, threatened to crack open his round pate if he came nigh them." When ex-President Adams was in Boston in the summer of 1831, Emerson was a fellow-guest with him at the home of Dr. Francis Parkman. In 1864 Emerson attended Hawthorne's funeral. A fellow mourner was ex-President Franklin Pierce, whom Emerson despised; he wrote: "Longfellow, Lowell, Holmes,

Agassiz, Hoar, Dwight, Whipple, Norton, Alcott, Hillard, Fields, Judge Thomas, and I attended the hearse as pall-bearers. Franklin Pierce was with the family." Through Charles Sumner, Emerson met Abraham Lincoln in February, 1862: "The President impressed me more favorably than I had hoped. A frank, sincere, well-meaning man, with a lawyer's habit of mind, good clear statement of his fact; correct enough, not vulgar, as described, but with a sort of boyish cheerfulness, or that kind of sincerity and jolly good meaning that our class meetings on Commencement Days show, in telling our old stories over. When he has made his remark, he looks up at you with great satisfaction, and shows all his white teeth, and laughs."

Perhaps the most illustrious near friend of Emerson was Daniel Webster, about whom there are dozens of journal entries. At first Emerson admired Webster's oratorical ability. Hearing Webster on the occasion of the deaths of Adams and Jefferson, Emerson at twenty-three wrote as follows: "Never, I think, were the awful charms of person, manners and voice outdone. For though in the beginning unpromising, and in other parts imperfect, in what was truly grand he fully realized the boldest conception of eloquence." But in October, 1841, Emerson registered discontent: "I saw Webster on the street,—but he was changed since I saw him last,—black as a thunder-cloud, and careworn. . . . I did not wonder that he depressed his eyes when he saw me, and would not meet my face. The cankerworms have crawled to the topmost bough of the wild elm and swing down from that. No wonder the elm is a little uneasy." By February, 1843, Emerson, still praising the man's appearance and thunderous eloquence, registered prophetic condemnation of Webster: "He has misused the opportunity of making himself the darling of the American world in all coming time by abstaining from putting himself at the head of the Anti-slavery interest, by standing for New England and for man against the bullying and barbarism of the South." In June, 1847, Emerson contented himself to remark of Webster merely that "his great proportions only expos[e] his defect." From this specific observation Emerson damningly generalizes as follows: "America seems to have immense resources, land, men, milk, butter, cheese, timber, and iron, but it is a village littleness;—village squabble and rapacity characterize its policy. It is a great strength on a basis of weakness." It is little wonder, then, that Emerson penned hundreds of angry words about the Fugitive Slave Law under the general heading of "Bad Times," in May, 1851. The following are representative and shake with indignation: "Mr. Webster has deliberately taken out his name from all the files of honor in which he had enrolled it,— from all association with liberal, virtuous, and philanthropic men, and read his recantation on his knees at Richmond and Charleston." The same long passage includes violent condemnation of other fallen greats, including Rufus Choate and Edward Everett, who displeased Emerson by arguing legalistically and forensically for the odious slave law.

A skillful politician always admired by Emerson was Charles Sumner, whom he succinctly describes in his journal in July, 1869, as "a brave, perfectly honest, and well-instructed man with social culture and relation to all eminent persons. Diligent and able workman, without humor, but with persevering study while reading, excellent memory, high sense of honor, disdaining any bribe, any compliances, and incapable of falsehood. His singular advantages of person, of manners, and a statesman's conversation, impress every one favorably."

As for other eminent associates, aside from men of letters,

Emerson recorded his impressions of the scientist Louis Agassiz, the painter Washington Allston, the abolitionist John Brown, the Unitarian minister William Ellery Channing the younger, and the sculptor Horatio Greenough, among dozens of others less luminous. Of Agassiz we read: "He is a man to be thankful for, always cordial, full of facts, with unsleeping observation, and perfectly communicative." Saying that "Allston's pictures are Elysian; fair, serene, but unreal," Emerson bracketed the painter with other American men of art and then added, in a famous terse line, "all lack nerve and dagger." Early in 1857 Emerson recorded simply: "Captain John Brown of Kansas gave a good account of himself in the Town Hall, last night, to a meeting of citizens." While walking one fine autumn day with W. E. Channing the younger, Emerson observed that quick-changing nature is often "on the gallop"; seeing a connection with his friend, he went on: "Incessant whirl. And 'tis the same with my companion's genius. You must carry a stenographic press in your pocket to save his commentaries on things and men, or they are irrecoverable. I tormented my memory just now in vain to restore a witty criticism of his, yesterday, on a book." In his mid-sixties, Emerson looked back upon his many intellectual associates and wrote with moving brevity of the sculptor Greenough, among several other stimulating persons: "Horatio Greenough shone, but one only listened to him . . ."

A list of Emerson's American literary acquaintances would include almost everyone of consequence from 1830 to 1865 except Edgar Allan Poe and Herman Melville. Emerson had only a routine respect for the polite Boston writers. For example, the following apparent praise of Oliver Wendell Holmes is representative of Emerson's opinions in general of the Brahmins and is undercut by implicit criticism: "What a convivial talent is that of Wendell Holmes. He is still at his Club, when he travels in search of his wounded son; has the same delight in his perceptions, in his wit, in its effect, which he watches as a belle the effect of her beauty; would still hold each companion fast by his spritely, sparkling, widely-allusive talk, as at the [Saturday] Club table; tastes all his own talent, calculates every stroke, and yet the fountain is unfailing, the wit excellent, the *savoir faire* and *savoir parler* admirable." To be sure, Emerson gracefully praises James Russell Lowell for his 1862 *Biglow Papers*: "We will not again disparage America, now that we have seen what men it will bear. What a certificate of good elements in the soil, climate, and institutions is Lowell, whose admirable verses I have just read!"

But in general Emerson was more excited by those American authors whose genius was generally not recognized until after his time. The best example is Henry David Thoreau, concerning whom there are nearly thirty entries in Perry's edition of the *Journals*. Emerson plainly saw Thoreau's worth, as a writer, a nature-lover, and a man. We read this 1842 entry: "Last night Henry Thoreau read me verses which pleased, if not by beauty of particular lines, yet by the honest truth, and by the length of flight and strength of wing; for most of our poets are only writers of lines or of epigrams. These of Henry's at least have rude strength, and we do not come to the bottom of the mine." Then Emerson added a line which he used twenty years later in his eulogy of Thoreau: "Their fault is, that the gold does not yet flow pure, but is drossy and crude." In the late 1840's Emerson read and delighted in Thoreau's "Katahdin," decades before anyone else saw its value: "We have not had since ten years a

pamphlet which I have saved to bind! and here at last is
. . . Henry Thoreau's *Ascent of Katahdin*." Shortly after his
friend's untimely death, Emerson generously wrote:

> In reading Henry Thoreau's journal, I am very sensible
> of the vigor of his constitution. That oaken strength
> which I noted whenever he walked, or worked, or sur-
> veyed wood-lots, the same unhesitating hand with
> which a field-laborer accosts a piece of work, which I
> should shun as a waste of strength, Henry shows in his
> literary task. He has muscle, and ventures on and per-
> forms feats which I am forced to decline. In reading
> him, I find the same thought, the same spirit that is in
> me, but he takes a step beyond, and illustrates by ex-
> cellent images that which I should have conveyed in a
> sleepy generality.

Finally, in June of 1871, Emerson enshrined Thoreau, with a
few others, in a list entitled "My Men." Among notable contemporary writers, only Carlyle, Lowell, Alcott, and Holmes
are also included.

Emerson also privately praised Margaret Fuller, Jones
Very, and Walt Whitman, all of whom are more highly regarded now than they were a century ago. He puts Margaret
Fuller in awesome company in this passage: "I know nobody
among my contemporaries except Carlyle who writes with
any sinew and vivacity comparable to Plutarch and Montaigne. . . . I cannot now read Webster's speeches. Fuller and
[Sir Thomas] Browne and Milton are quick, but the list is
soon ended. Goethe seems to be well alive, no pedant. Luther
too." The few entries concerning Very are not particularly
quotable, but they show Emerson's admiration for the man's
sincerity and poetic expression, and sympathy for his mental
unbalance. Emerson's qualified respect for Whitman is well

known; in the journal he noted at one point: ". . . one must thank Walt Whitman for service to American literature in the Appalachian enlargement of his outline and treatment."

Like most people, Emerson had his blind spot when it came to viewing his contemporaries. Along with most Americans until the 1920's if not later, he ignored Herman Melville. Moreover, his journal makes no mention of Poe, whom he elsewhere dismissed as "the jingle-man." Hawthorne's gloomy view of life he deplored, instinctively, as it may be supposed he did Melville's too. In 1842 he enigmatically penned this into his journal: "Nathaniel Hawthorne's reputation as a writer is a very pleasing fact, because his writing is not good for anything, and this is a tribute to the man." In conversation much later, he branded Hawthorne's *Marble Faun* as "mere mush." And later, after the novelist's death, Emerson curiously recorded this note: "I thought him a greater man than any of his works betray, that there was still a great deal of work in him, and that he might one day show a purer power."

The journals are crammed with comments on the personalities and works of past great writers, including among others Plato, Plutarch, Dante, Shakespeare, Bacon, Milton, Montaigne, Rabelais, Voltaire, and Pope. Emerson reserves his highest praise for very few: "If I reckon up my debts by particulars to English books, how fast they reduce themselves to a few authors, and how conspicuous Shakespeare, Bacon, and Milton become . . ." Montaigne he loves: "With all my heart I embrace the grand old sloven. He pricks and stings the sense of virtue in men . . ." The few entries on Plutarch are disappointing, since it is well known that Emerson revered his *Morals* more than almost any other literary work; in fact, in his late essay "Books" he says that "Plutarch cannot be spared from the smallest library; first because he is so readable, which is much; then that he is medicinal and in-vigorating." Emerson did not like all "great" writers. For example, he once comprehensively castigated an important trio: "Pope and Johnson and Addison write as if they had never seen the face of the country, but had only read of trees and rivers in books." And his dislike of Voltaire is revealing; visiting the chateau of that "king of the scorners" near Geneva, he grudgingly recorded these words: "Yet it would be a sin against faith and philosophy to exclude Voltaire from tolera-tion. He did his work as the bustard and tarantula do theirs."

Among contemporary European writers Emerson obvi-ously accorded Carlyle the highest place. He also praised the humanitarian quality of Charles Dickens: "The next genera-tion will thank Dickens for showing so many mischiefs which parliaments and Christianities had not been strong enough to remove." He reluctantly wrote the following in 1852: "Words-worth, Coleridge, Tennyson, Carlyle, and Macaulay cannot be matched in America." But he skewered *In Memoriam* aptly: "Tennyson's *In Memoriam* is the commonplaces of condo-lences among good Unitarians in the first week of mourning. The consummate skill of the versification is the sole merit." Late in his life, Emerson was suddenly made aware of John Ruskin's virtues; when he was sixty-eight he wrote: "Ruskin is a surprise to me. This old book, *Two Paths*, is original, acute, thoroughly informed, and religious."

All these writers and their important works passed in review before Emerson's steady vision, and the ways in which they stimulated him are usually recorded carefully in his journals.

The big events which occurred in America during the period of Emerson's journals include the Missouri Com-promise, the advent of Jacksonian democracy, the Mexican War, the California gold rush, the Compromise of 1850, the

Fugitive Slave Law, the Lincoln-Douglas Debates, John Brown's raid on Harper's Ferry, and the Civil War and its aftermath. By the time of the age which Mark Twain sardonically called "gilded," Emerson had gently drifted into senility; so his journals after about 1872 are of little value. They trail to an end in 1875.

In his journals, Emerson regularly associated big events with representative men. Thus, instead of philosophizing on Jacksonian democracy, he writes of "the fine military energy of Jackson in his presidency." One of Emerson's responses to the Mexican War was this: "Mr. Webster told them how much the war cost, that was his protest, but voted the war, and sends his son to it. They calculated rightly on Mr. Webster. My friend Mr. Thoreau has gone to jail rather than pay his tax. On him they could not calculate. The Abolitionists denounce the war and give much time to it, but they pay the tax. [So did Emerson.]" California's gold interested him less than its weather: "The attraction and superiority of California are in its days. It has better days, and more of them, than any other country." He gave vent to his strongest language on the occasion of the Compromise of 1850 with its attendant Fugitive Slave Law, which like the Mexican War he associated with Webster: "The word *liberty* in the mouth of Mr. Webster sounds like the word *love* in the mouth of a courtezan." Then: "What a moment was lost when Judge [Lemuel] Shaw declined to affirm the unconstitutionality of the Fugitive Slave Law!" And finally: "This filthy enactment was made in the nineteenth century, by people who could read and write. I will not obey it, by God." The Kansas-Nebraska Act of 1854 occasioned this entry: "There is nobody in Washington who can explain this Nebraska business to the people,—nobody of weight. And nobody of any importance on the bad side. It is only done by [Senator Stephen A.]

Douglas and his accomplices by calculation on the brutal ignorance of the people, upon the wretched masses of Pennsylvania, Indiana, Illinois, Kentucky, and so on, people who
can't read or know anything beyond what the village democrat tells them." After a year of the Civil War, Emerson
grumbled in a letter to his brother William, reprinted in part
in the journals, about his failing royalties and annuities, and
then added stoically: "But far better that this grinding should
go on, bad and worse, than we be driven by any impatience
into a hasty peace, or any peace restoring the old rottenness."
Emerson recorded one free man's opposition to the Civil War
of abolition, and a canny refutation thereof: "George Francis
Train said in a public speech in New York, 'Slavery is a
divine institution.' 'So is hell,' exclaimed an old man in the
crowd." By the end of the Civil War, the journals show a
distinct lessening of interest in great public events. Emerson
in 1869 spoke of his own "failing memory," which perhaps
was accompanied by a diminution of mental powers generally. In 1870 he wrote: "Very much afflicted in these days
with stupor:—acute attacks when ever a visit is proposed or
made." This stupor probably eclipsed much of his former
interest in national events.

In addition to persons, books, and events, Emerson
lavished attention in his journals upon emotions and ideas of
many sorts. It is a joy to leaf through his pages and watch
his sinewy mind grappling with abstractions important and
less so. His youthful humility in the face of his wife Ellen's
young love and his duties at the Second Church of Boston is
touching: "Whilst I enjoy the luxury of an unmeasured
affection for an object so deserving of it all, and who re-
quites it all,—I am called by an ancient and respectable church
to become its pastor. I recognize in these events . . . the hand
of my heavenly father." After Ellen's death, Emerson mourned

and prayed, and then wrote: "There is that which passes away and never returns. This miserable apathy, I know, may wear off. I almost fear when it will. Old duties will present themselves with no more repulsive face. . . . Again I shall be amused . . . But will the dead be restored to me? . . . Shall I ever again be able to connect the face of outward nature, the mists of the morn, the star of eve, the flowers, and all poetry, with the heart and life of an enchanting friend? No." In 1861, rightly seeing that he was approaching old age, he stoically recorded the following thoughts, which have been misunderstood out of their context: "*Advantages of old age.* I reached the other day the end of my fifty-seventh year, and am easier in my mind than hitherto. I could never give much reality to evil and pain. But now when my wife says perhaps this tumor on your shoulder is a cancer, I say, What if it is?" Even earlier, at the age of only forty-three, he could write with Olympian contentment: "When summer opens, I see how fast it matures, and fear it will be short; but after the heats of July and August, I am reconciled, like one who has had his swing, to the cool of autumn. So will it be with the coming of death."

The character and influence of Christ thoroughly engaged Emerson's mind. Sympathetically regarding the Sermon on the Mount as the product "of the mind contemning the phenomenal world," Emerson went on as follows: "The Understanding can make nothing of it. 'Tis all nonsense. The Reason affirms its absolute verity." Later he noted that "the discovery of Jesus" is "that God must be sought within, not without." The enormous influence of Christ intrigued Emerson, who when Ernst Renan published his *Vie de Jésus* recorded humbly: "When I wrote *Representative Men,* I felt that Jesus was the 'Representative Man' whom I ought to sketch; but the task required great gifts,—steadfast insight and perfect temper; else, the consciousness of want of sympathy in the audience would make one petulant or sore, in spite of himself."

Any person perusing the journals will see that Emerson touches upon innumerable great and homely topics, but almost never are his comments simply of transient value. For example, can we not apply the following casual remarks to our present-day post-Bomb misery? "Don't trust children with edge tools. Don't trust man, great God, with more power than he has, until he has learned to use that little better. . . . Put a button on the foil till the young fencers have learned not to put each other's eyes out." And is not Emerson's criticism of the Brook Farm communal experiment applicable, with a little modernizing, to the concept of the welfare state? He wrote that "this scheme was arithmetic and comfort: . . . the rage in our poverty and politics to live rich and gentlemanlike, an anchor to leeward against a change of weather . . ." A little later he added this deadly-accurate prophecy: "Brook Farm will show a few noble victims, who act and suffer with temper and proportion, but the larger part will be slight adventurers and will shirk work." No airy dreamer, Emerson admired the practical person who could get things done: "When Edward and I struggled in vain to drag our big calf into the barn, the Irish girl put her finger into the calf's mouth, and led her in directly." And although Emerson wrote pure enough English, he dearly loved forceful common speech: "The language of the street is always strong. What can describe the folly and emptiness of scolding like the word *jawing?* I feel too the force of the double negative, though clear contrary to our grammar rules. And I confess to some pleasure from the stinging rhetoric of a rattling oath in the mouth of truckmen and teamsters. How laconic and brisk it is . . . Cut these words and they would bleed; they are vascular and alive; they walk and run." (Most of this last sentence he later used in his essay "Montaigne" to describe the great French writer's diction.)

Emerson is not a wild humorist, but nonetheless his journals contain a few funny passages. For example, humorously judging one of his own lectures as competent but lacking in necessary transitions, he records the following: "I found when I had finished my new lecture that it was a very good house, only the architect had unfortunately omitted the stairs." Well aware that he lugged his satchel full of lectures about the country later in life mostly for cold cash, he could put it thus amusingly: " 'Twas tedious, the squalor and obstructions of travel; the advantage of their offers at Chicago made it necessary to go; in short, this dragging of a decorous old gentleman out of home and out of position to this juvenile career was tantamount to this,—'I'll bet you fifty dollars a day that you will not leave your library, and wade and ride and run and suffer all manner of indignities and stand up for an hour each night reading in a hall'; and I answered, 'I'll bet I will.' I do it and win the $900." He recognized his own enigmatic qualities. When he was past seventy and back home from Egypt, he noted the following anecdote: "Mrs. Helen Bell, it seems, was asked, 'What do you think the Sphinx said to Mr. Emerson?' 'Why,' replied Mrs. Bell, 'the Sphinx probably said to him, "You're another." ' " Perhaps the funniest passage in all of the journals is this one, which is worthy of a light-hearted Mark Twain: "Dr. Ripley prays for rain with great explicitness on Sunday, and on Monday the showers fell. When I spoke of the speed with which his prayers were answered, the good man looked modest."

One final point—and an important one it is—concerning

the journals. When he was only thirty, Emerson himself sagely described the nature and purpose of his notebooks: "This book is my Savings Bank. I grow richer because I have somewhere to deposit my earnings; and fractions are worth more to me because corresponding fractions are waiting here that shall be made integers by their addition." From time to time all through his active life he deposited in the savings bank of his journals an unrefined nugget, his groat's worth of wit, a handful of shining coins, and occasionally whole little moneybags of polished thoughts. When it came time to assemble notes for a lecture, or to put together an essay or a poem, he turned to his journals and found that his work was partly done already. For example, home from a seaside vacation in July, 1856, Emerson penned this shimmering prose:

> Returned from Pigeon Cove, where we have made acquaintance with the sea, for seven days. 'Tis a noble friendly power, and seemed to say to me, "Why so late and slow to come to me? Am I not always thy proper summer home? Is not my voice thy needful music: my breath, thy healthful climate in the heats; my touch, thy cure? Lie down on my warm ledges and learn that a very little hut is all you need. I have made thy architecture superfluous, and it is paltry beside mine. Here are twenty Romes and Ninevehs and Karnacs in ruins together, obelisk and pyramid and giant's causeway,— here they all are prostrate or half piled."
> And behold the sea, the opaline, plentiful and strong, yet beautiful as the rose or the rainbow, full of food, nourisher of men, purger of the world, creating a sweet climate, and, in its unchangeable ebb and flow,

and in its beauty at a few furlongs, giving a hint of that which changes not, and is perfect.

Seven or eight years later, when the time seemed right, Emerson turned back to this beautiful passage and to the mood which evoked it, and composed his fine poem "Seashore," the first half of which is taken almost verbatim from the journals. And so with the initial impulse for his matchless poem "Days." In the journal for May, 1847, we read: "The days come and go like muffled and veiled figures sent from a distant friendly party, but they say nothing, and if we do not use the gifts they bring, they carry them as silently away." Furthermore, scholars have traced image after image and paragraph after paragraph from the major essays back to brief passages in the journals. Thus "Compensation" (1841) grew in part out of thoughts behind such lines from the journals as the following: "All things are double one against another, said Solomon. The whole of what we know is a system of compensations. Every defect in one manner is made up in another. Every suffering is rewarded; every sacrifice is made up; every debt is paid [1826]." "Is not the law of compensation perfect? It holds as far as we can see. Different gifts to different individuals, but with a mortgage of responsibility on every one. 'The gods *sell* all things.' . . . I have nothing charactered in my brain that outlives this word Compensation. Old Stubler . . . said to me, that, if a man sacrificed his impurity, purity should be the price with which it would be paid; if a man gave up his hatred, he should be rewarded with love—'tis the same old melody and it sounds through the vast of being [1831]." "There is no material show so splendid, no poem so musical as the great law of Compensation in our moral nature [1834]." And "The Teacher that

I look for and await shall enunciate with more precision and universality, with piercing poetic insight those beautiful yet severe compensations that give to moral nature an aspect of mathematical science [1835]."

It is the same with many other essays and poems. Into the savings bank of his journals, Emerson deposited countless thoughts, later to withdraw them with interest and put them into circulation as literature.

The Journals of Ralph Waldo Emerson, then, are fascinating to read. In them we can find evidence of his thoughts on many illustrious colleagues and friends, on numerous writers and their works, on the leading American politicians and thinkers, and on the themes and ideas which he wove into his most representative essays and poems.

IV. ESSAYS

Emerson is most characteristic and popular in his essays. A survey of more than twenty recent books containing selections of his prose works reveals that the following have been the most popular, and popular in the order given here: "The American Scholar" (a lecture which has already been discussed), "Self-Reliance," "Nature" (a short book but hardly longer than a long lecture or essay), "The Poet," "Experience," "Thoreau" (a eulogy already discussed), "The Over-Soul," "Divinity School Address" (a lecture already discussed), "Illusions," "Fate," "Politics," "Compensation," "Montaigne," "Plato," "Education" (a lecture already discussed), and "New England Reformers." Other anthologies and books in which Emerson's prose is represented may have other essays, but most of the above titles are much more important than any others.

Nature

Nature was Emerson's first book. It was published in 1836 in less than one hundred pages. Although it has never been popular, it is highly significant and may be regarded as a manifesto of American Transcendentalism. Carlyle was absolutely right when he called it "the Foundation or Ground-Plan on which you may build." "Nature" contains the first tentative expression of most of Emerson's later ideas.

"Nature" is in nine parts: Introduction, I. Nature, II. Commodity, III. Beauty, IV. Language, V. Discipline, VI.

Idealism, VII. Spirit, and VIII. Prospects. Everything through "Discipline" is a unified description of physical nature and its effects upon the mind of man. The last three parts less successfully switch to a consideration of ideal, non-material nature.

Introduction—Emerson suggests that instead of looking back to history and biography, and thus seeing nature indirectly, we should "enjoy an original relation to the universe," trusting that we can find our own answers to our own questions: ". . . whatever curiosity the order of things has awakened in our minds, the order of things can satisfy." The aim of all science is to explain nature, but much which is "not only unexplained but inexplicable" remains, for example, "language, sleep, madness, dreams, beasts, sex." Philosophy tells us that "the universe is composed of Nature and the Soul." The "not me" of the universe—nature, art, other people, even our own bodies—we shall call Nature. All else is the Soul.

I. Nature—The only way a man can be truly alone is to get away from society and also from books, and to commune with an aspect of nature, for example, the stars. "If the stars should appear one night in a thousand years, how would men believe and adore; and preserve for many generations the remembrance of the city of God which had been shown! But every night come out these envoys of beauty, and light the universe with their admonishing smile." Nature is inexhaustibly curious, its elements coalescing into a poetic, inaccessible, but observable whole. Unfortunately, however, few adults have more than a superficial, transitory relationship with nature. "The sun illuminates only the eye of the man, but shines into the eye and the heart of the child." The true lover of nature is the one whose "inward and outward senses are still truly adjusted to each other; who has retained the spirit of infancy even into the era of manhood." This sort of delight in nature is rare. Emerson tells us frankly that he has known it. "Crossing a bare common, in snow puddles, at twilight, under a clouded sky, without having in my thoughts any occurrence of special good fortune, I have enjoyed a perfect exhilaration. I am glad to the brink of fear." Anyone can go into the woods and shed his skin of adult years and cares like a snake. Nature appeals to the perennial youth in us. Then Emerson again memorably expresses his sense of ecstasy and trust in nature. "There I feel that nothing can befall me in life,—no disgrace, no calamity (leaving me my eyes), which nature cannot repair. Standing on the bare ground,—my head bathed in the blithe air, and uplifted into infinite space,—all mean egotism vanishes. I become a transparent eyeball; I am nothing; I see all; the currents of the Universal Being circulate through me; I am part or parcel of God." The finest delight accorded man by nature is the suggestion that the power to produce pleasure resides neither in nature nor alone in man but in the harmony of the two. Further, "Nature always wears the colors of the spirit," so that to a melancholy person nature is somehow less grand.

II. Commodity—by commodity Emerson means all the advantages to our senses and persons which we owe to nature, that is, all sensations and all materials. More than this, nature shows man various processes which his inventiveness causes him to imitate. "The useful arts are reproductions or new combinations by the wit of man, of the same natural benefactors. He no longer waits for favoring gales, but by means of steam, he realizes the fable of Æolus's bag, and carries the two and thirty winds in the boiler of his boat."

III. Beauty—"A nobler want of man is served by nature, namely, the love of Beauty." The Greeks were right in using one word—κόσμος—to mean both world and beauty. All the elements in the world flow together into "outline, color, motion, and group" which has beauty. Every object in nature, even a corpse, is beautiful if it is seen in the proper light. Beauty is of three types—physical, spiritual, and intellectual. "First, the simple perception of natural forms is a delight." Physical nature is shot through with wondrous beauty. "The leafless trees become spires of flame in the sunset, with the blue east for their background, and the stars of the dead calices of flowers, and every withered stem and stubble rimed with frost, contribute something to the mute music." Even winter is replete with its graceful beauty, as is every shallow little river. But natural beauty is best of all when it is a part of or a setting for man's daily working life. "Go out of the house to see the moon, and 'tis mere tinsel; it will not please as when its light shines upon your necessary journey." Higher than physical beauty is spiritual beauty. Emerson rather naively adds that "Beauty is the mark God sets upon virtue." (Hollywood surely knows better than this.) And of Leonidas and his men, Arnold Winkelried, Columbus, Sir Henry Vane, and Lord Russell, for example, Emerson asks, "are not these heroes entitled to add the beauty of the scene to the beauty of the deed? . . . can we separate the man from the living picture? . . . Ever does natural beauty steal in like air, and envelope great actions." So natural beauty is evoked by and complements heroic and spiritually admirable conduct. The highest type of beauty is intellectual, by which Emerson means the charming order of things in nature as perceived by the intellect. We perceive physical and spiritual beauty, and then understand its patterns. "This love of beauty is Taste." The mind recognizes that beauty is the common denominator of all things in nature, which coalesce into meaningful artistic wholes. "Nothing is quite beautiful alone; nothing but is beautiful in the whole. A single object is only so far beautiful as it suggests this universal grace. The poet, the painter, the sculptor, the musician, the architect, seek each to concentrate this radiance of the world on one point. . . . Thus is Art a nature passed through the alembic of man." The soul desires beauty, and the world exists to satisfy this desire. "Beauty, in its largest and profoundest sense, is one expression for the universe. . . . Truth, and goodness, and beauty, are but different faces of the same All." Finally, Emerson states that natural, outward beauty is not ultimate but is rather "the herald of inward and eternal beauty, and is not alone a solid and satisfactory good. It must stand as a part, and not as yet the last or highest expression of the final cause of Nature."

IV. Language—In addition to providing commodity and beauty, nature is the source of all language for man. Here Emerson rather ramblingly develops the notions that words are signs of natural facts, that natural facts symbolize spiritual facts, and that nature is the symbol of spirit. All our words come directly or indirectly from nature. "Every word which is used to express a moral or intellectual fact, if traced to its root, is found to be borrowed from some material appearance." But more important to the Transcendentalist is this: "It is not words only that are emblematic; it is things which are emblematic. Every natural fact is a symbol of some spiritual fact. Every appearance in nature corresponds to some state of the mind, and that state of the mind can only be described by presenting that natural appearance as its picture." Thus, for a few examples, *lamb* suggests innocence; *snake,* subtle spite; and "flowers express to us the delicate affections." Everything physical is symbolic of something nonmaterial, and "man is an analogist, and studies relations in all objects." Thus man and nature are interdependent and complementary. Next Emerson naively posits a theory of language. "As we go back in history, language becomes more picturesque, until its infancy, when it is all poetry; or all spiritual facts are represented by natural symbols." ·But as man fell from his original naturally pure state, his language inevitably was corrupted. There are two remedies: "wise men pierce this rotten diction and fasten words again to visible things," and they also recognize "the advantage which the country-life possesses . . . over the artificial and curtailed life of cities." We should realize that too often we use words of noble pedigrees to express commonplace notions. Too seldom are we aware that our simple sayings have not only a physical but an ethical import: ". . . the memorable words of history and the proverbs of nations consist usually of a natural fact, selected as a picture or parable of a moral truth." Examples concern rolling stones, a bird in the hand, the camel's back, and so on.

V. Discipline—All elements in nature educate the understanding and the reason to an awareness that matter and mind are linked. Nature disciplines the understanding as to intellectual truths. All events in life are educative, even simple ones concerning property and poverty. "Debt, grinding debt, whose iron face the widow, the orphan, and the sons of genius fear and hate;—debt, which consumes so much time, which so cripples and disheartens a great spirit with cares that seem so base, is a preceptor whose lessons cannot be foregone, and is needed most by those who suffer from it most." The confusing clutter of things in nature challenges the thinker to see differences and similarities. Science has taught us much, but "we are [still] impressed and even daunted by the immense Universe to be explored." Then Emerson romantically suggests that all natural processes instruct us in morals: ". . . every animal function from the sponge up to Hercules, shall hint or thunder to man the laws of right and wrong, and echo the Ten Commandments." All these diverse lessons point to "the unity of Nature,—the unity in variety." This unity becomes conspicuous when one studies apparently varied forms of matter, life, words, and actions. Each such element is a microcosm, containing all the world in it.

VI. Idealism—It was at this point in his long essay that Emerson first ran into trouble. On August 8, 1836, a month before the little book was published, he wrote his brother William as follows: "The book of Nature still lies on the table. There is, as always, one crack in it not easy to be soldered or welded, but if this week I should be left alone . . . I may finish it." The fissure separates Emerson's consideration of nature as tangible and nature as simply a reflection of the mind. Emerson does not satisfactorily weld or solder together the parts dealing with matter and those dealing with the soul. However, if Emerson cannot reconcile mind and matter, he is in good company. At any rate, in the section called "Idealism" he asks whether matter exists independent of the human mind, only to answer by pragmatically saying "what is the difference . . . ? Whether nature enjoy a substantial existence without, or is only in the apocalypse of the mind, it is alike useful and alike venerable to me." He goes on to say that God never jokes with us, that natural laws seem permanent whether they really are or not, and that "the question of the absolute existence of nature still remains open." To the mere understanding, nature appears to be fixed and absolute, but reason "tends to relax this despotism of the senses which binds us to nature as if we were a part of it, and shows us nature aloof, and, as it were, afloat." Reason sees all there is in nature but in addition grace, expression, cause, and spirit. Then Emerson makes four points concerning idealistic philosophy. First, if we change our point of view in nature, the appearance of nature itself changes drastically. Thus nature conspires with us to make us feel that nature itself is not fixed but is only

apparent. Second, the poetic imagination ranges through nature and changes it at will. "This transfiguration which all
material objects undergo through the passion of the poet,—
this power which he exerts to dwarf the great, to magnify
the small,—might be illustrated by a thousand examples. . ."
Third, whereas the poet seeks beauty and the philosopher
truth, the two "postpone . . . the apparent order and relations
of things to the empire of thought." Philosophical ideas of
truth are poetically beautiful, and like poetry pervade and
dissolve matter. Fourth, "Intellectual science has been observed to beget invariably a doubt of the existence of matter."
Ideas are more permanent than matter and are often free of
it. They elevate us fearlessly above mere matter. Then, having
expatiated lengthily on idealism, Emerson rather weakly says,
"But I own there is something ungrateful in expanding too
curiously the particulars of the general proposition, that all
culture tends to imbue us with idealism," desirable and
flattering though it is to the mind.

VII. Spirit—Any true theory of nature and man must
eventually address itself to spirit. The best that nature can
teach us is the lesson of worship. "We can see God in the
coarse and . . . distant phenomena of matter; but when we
try to define and describe himself, both language and thought
desert us . . . That essence refuses to be recorded in propo-
sitions, but when man has worshipped him intellectually,
the noblest ministry of nature is to stand as the apparition
of God." Such a spiritual view makes matter a phenomenon
rather than a substance, a something behind and through
which spirit is ever present. Awareness of this fact makes
the human will serene through its being inviolable by matter.

VII. Prospects—Since "The foundations of man are
not in matter, but in spirit," we should rely more on our

intuition "than [on] a hundred concerted experiments," should pay more attention to guesses and dreams. Emerson goes on in this way: "I cannot greatly honor minuteness in details, so long as there is no hint to explain the relation between things and thoughts." All specific material designs should ultimately be seen as "faint copies of an invisible archetype. Nor has science sufficient humanity, so long as the naturalist overlooks that wonderful congruity which subsists between man and the natural world." Because he has both head and heart, man is lord of that world and sees something of himself in everything, great and small, therein. As George Herbert says of man, "His eyes dismount the highest star," and "More servants wait on man / Than he'll take notice of." Plato reasons that "poetry comes nearer to vital truth than history." In conclusion, Emerson quotes "a certain poet" (probably himself) to the effect that "man is a god in ruins," and must awake and grow again into his proper place. "Meantime, in the thick darkness, there are not wanting gleams of a better light,—occasional examples of the action of man upon nature with his entire force,—with reason as well as understanding." Such "gleams" include miracles which are traditional in all early nations, the history of Jesus, principles which work religious and political changes, the enthusiasm of mystics, hypotism, prayer, and so on. But each of us must continue the good work of restoring the unity of the world by becoming unified with himself again, by gaining wisdom through prayer, by recognizing the miraculous in common and everyday phenomena and events—time, the seasons, womanhood, sleep—and by seeing poetry in lowly facts. When we do this, "Then shall come to pass what my poet said: 'Nature is not fixed but fluid. Spirit alters, moulds, makes it. The immobility or bruteness of nature is the absence of spirit; to pure spirit it is fluid, it is volatile, it is obedient.

Every spirit builds itself a house, and beyond its house a world, and beyond its world a heaven. Know then that the world exists for you. For you is the phenomenon perfect. What we are, that only can we see. . . . Build therefore your own world. . . .'" If we do so, then we will easily slip into man's kingdom over nature.

To conclude, in "Nature" Emerson suggests that each of us should establish an original relationship with nature, realizing that it needs our perceptive feelings and thoughts to complete it. Nature provides us with senses and with processes to emulate, with evidence of physical and spiritual and intellectual beauty, with limitless sources for words and symbols expressing Transcendental meanings, and with lessons which educate the reason and the understanding. At the same time, the relationship of inner and outer nature is such that the metaphysician can legitimately develop an idealistic philosophy, arguing that outer nature depends for its very existence upon the perceiving, creating mind and serene spirit of man. This being the case, we should rejoice in the organic fluidity of things all about us and build our love of the common and ordinary into a new and poetic kingdom of man.

Stylistically "Nature" is a combination of impassioned lyricism and unassimilated abstractions. Its poetic prose is a delight; but its compressed idealism, while moving enough emotionally, is hard to paraphrase or even, at times, to follow. The purpose and influence of "Nature" are significant. Emerson aimed to deny eighteenth-century Deism, which made the universe into a tidy materialistic machine, like a terribly efficient clock, and substituted for it a poetic vision of the cosmos as a vibrant, thrilling, changing organism. Nature thus became important not as a puzzling mechanism for the tinkering scientist but as a treasury of symbols and a metaphysical challenge to the creative mind of man. And the essay "Nature," as a Transcendental manifesto, helped establish the Transcendental Club, the *Dial* magazine, and communal farm experiments, and in addition influenced the thinking of innumerable Transcendental friends of its author.

Self-Reliance

Published in *Essays, First Series,* in 1841, the tremendously popular essay "Self-Reliance" brilliantly overstates the typical Emersonian thesis that one should trust himself. Emerson made this point in "The American Scholar" for man thinking, and again in "Divinity School Address" for the would-be minister. Here he universalizes his message. First he almost tediously sermonizes on his text—"Trust thyself: every heart vibrates to that iron string." Then he shows that he means no juvenile and irresponsible self-indulgence but rather a mature if independently achieved reliance upon the source of the developed self, namely, God. Emerson points the main part of his essay toward the following conclusion: "Nothing can bring you peace but the triumph of principles."

It must be said at once that the essay "Self-Reliance" is an eclectic ramble. Emerson derived most of it from journal entries and passages from his lectures going back almost a decade. Therefore it has little development and less unity, aside from the fact that it is all about self-reliance.

The essay begins by pointing out that the highest merit of great writers whom we extol is that "they set at naught books and traditions, and spoke not what men, but that *they* thought." Sooner or later each educated person realizes that "he must take himself for better or worse as his portion." Everyone is an individual. Animals and children teach us this. "Infancy conforms to nobody . . ." We fancy that children rely only upon us, but when they get out of range they are self-reliant. "The nonchalance of boys who are sure of a dinner . . . is the healthy attitude for human nature." Children judge adults alarmingly fast. But society comes along and eclipses youthful independence and rewards the young for conformity. "Whoso would be a man, must be a nonconformist," Emerson argues instead, adding that at times he feels like rebuking the abolitionist and even feels like preaching the doctrine of hatred and refusing to be brotherly at all. He would go to prison if necessary for those with whom he feels a spiritual affinity, but he begrudges his contributions to "your miscellaneous popular charities," since they often only educate fools and provide "alms to sots." Surely it is better to retain one's independence while at the same time resisting the desire to leave town. Since conforming merely screens one, it is surely better for a person to let his individual work identify him rather than donning "the prison-uniform of the party."

Some people are reluctant to be themselves today and then be themselves again tomorrow in a different way, for fear that they will appear inconsistent. Emerson's famous answer: "Suppose you should contradict yourself; what then? . . . A foolish consistency is the hobgoblin of little minds, adored by little statesmen and philosophers and divines. With consistency a great soul has simply nothing to do." Far from worrying about being misunderstood, one should realize that "To be great is to be misunderstood" and that misunderstood persons are in the company of Pythagoras, Socrates, Jesus, Luther, Copernicus, Galileo, and Newton [and Emerson]. Make a little progress today, and tomorrow make a little progress in a somewhat different direction. "The voyage of the best ship is a zigzag line of a hundred tacks."

Now Emerson pauses to name again two of his hates—conformity and consistency—before going to his next topic, the transcendent importance of the individual. Think of certain individuals—Caesar, Fox, Wesley—and you will realize that "An institution is the lengthened shadow of one man." The common individual too should feel confident of his powers. The fable of the sot who awakens in the duke's castle and feels at home there is popular because "it symbolizes . . . the state of man, who is in the world a sort of sot, but now and then wakes up, excercises his reason and finds himself a true prince." We should be more confident. Heroes are heroic, but there is plenty of virtue left for us to show. We should all trust our instincts and intuitions, since they proceed from "the same [divine] source" from which emanate things, space, light, time, and all mankind. Imitate the roses which, glad to be alive, "make no reference to former roses or to better ones; they are for what they are; they exist with God to-day." "Life only avails, not the having lived." Each living thing in the universe paradoxically seeks both a self-relying maturity and a resolution "into the ever-blessed One." To satisfy both aims, stay home, remain free, avoid joining organizations which will influence and warp you, and be candid in exhibiting the resultant independence and power. At the same time, be aware that neither self-reliance nor liberty is license. We all have duties—to family, community, self. These duties must be discharged. "There are two confessionals, in one or the other of which we must be shriven. You may fulfill your round of duties by clearing yourself in the *direct,* or in the *reflex* way. . . . But I may also neglect this reflex standard and absolve me to myself. I have my own stern claims and perfect circle. It denies the name of duty to many offices that are called duties." Because of society pressure, it is hardest of all to be faithful to duties to oneself.

Next Emerson gives a semblance of organization to his essay by offering five separate bits of advice to the would-be self-reliant. He numbers the first four precepts. (1) Rely less on prayer than on action. Those who are discontent and pray lack self-reliance. Since regret is a kind of false prayer, regret only those things which you can do something about. (2) Place less faith in travel. The restless traveler forgets that "Travelling is a fool's paradise." In reality, "He carries ruins to ruins," since wherever he goes he takes himself along. (3) Avoid imitating; ". . . what is imitation but a travelling of the mind?" The American artist is especially guilty here, imitating the past, the distant, the Doric, and the Gothic. He should instead realize that "Beauty, convenience, grandeur of thought and quaint expression are as near to us as to any, and if the American artist will study with hope and love the precise thing to be done by him, considering the climate, the soil, the length of the day, the wants of the people, the habit and form of the government, he will create a house in which all these will find themselves fitted, and taste and sentiment will be satisfied also." (4) Realize that "Society never advances. It recedes as fast on one side as it gains on the other." Therefore rely on yourself for advancement, and not on ever-changing society. Emerson gives examples of loss which attends gain. "The civilized man has built a coach, but has lost the use of his feet." The accuracy of the almanac only means that the individual "does not know a star in the sky." Further, "His note-books impair his memory; his libraries overload his wit; the insurance-office increases the number of accidents; and it may be a question whether machinery does not encumber . . ." Here it suits Emerson's purpose anti-romantically to oppose the notion of progress and argue rhetorically but not very persuasively that "Society is a wave. The wave moves onward, but the water of which it is composed does not. . . . The persons who make up a nation to-day, next year die, and their experience dies with them."

And (5) place less reliance on property. We wrongly support religious, educational, and civil institutions because they are "guards of property"; and we foolishly judge others by what they have rather than by what they are.

Emerson suddenly concludes by urging each of us to avoid placing trust in party delegates, to avoid relying on others to support our own position, never to bet on Fortune's rolling wheel, but instead to trust our own knowledge of cause and effect. Finally, making it clear that he links self-reliance and reliance on the ultimate source of the best in self, Emerson closes as follows: "Nothing can bring you peace but yourself. Nothing can bring you peace but the triumph of principles."

Compensation

Although "Compensation" was published with "Self-Reliance" in *Essays, First Series,* in 1841, it goes back to journal entries in the 1820's and earlier to some of Emerson's first mature philosophical speculations. Like the concept of self-reliance, the theory of compensation is basic to an understanding of his thought; but whereas self-reliance is muscular and bracing, the notion that "every crime is punished, every virtue rewarded" strikes most modern readers as naive. The essay owes much to Emerson's reading in science; it is one thing, however, to recognize polarities and opposite reactions in the physical world, but quite another to suggest that a sinner's remorse can wash away the consequences of his sin. A hit-and-run driver's conscience may make him confess and teach him humility, but his victim still lies mangled for life, and only Pollyanna would say that the victim is better off because he has gained knowledge and sympathy through suffering. (Hawthorne's Clifford Pyncheon knew better.) "Compensation" is not often reprinted today. Nonetheless, many of its metaphors and epigrams are provocative for present-day readers of unusual refinement and ethical sensitivity.

Emerson begins with an unnaturalistic little epigraph, which goes in part:

> Fear not, then, thou child infirm,
> There's no god dare wrong a worm.
>
> .   .   .   .
>
> Hast not thy share? On wingèd feet,
> Lo! it rushes thee to meet.

Then he dramatically insists that, far from operating simply in the next world to reward suffering virtue and to punish successful vice, the law of compensation acts here and now. Then he turns to material polarity. "Polarity, or action and reaction, we meet in every part of nature; in darkness and light; in heat and cold; in the ebb and flow of waters; in male and female; in the inspiration and expiration of plants and animals; in the equation of quantity and quality in the fluids of the animal body; in the systole and diastole of the heart; in the undulations of fluids and of sound; in the centrifugal and centripetal gravity; in electricity, galvanism, and chemical affinity." He goes on platonically: "An inevitable dualism bisects nature, so that each thing is a half, and suggests another thing to make it whole; as, spirit, matter; man, woman; odd, even; subjective, objective; in, out; upper, under; motion, rest; yea, nay." Then he applies this to the condition of man. One who loses, gains; one who gains, loses. An eternal process of leveling goes on, and "the President has paid dear for his White House." This same leveling applies to "cities and nations. . . . Things refuse to be mismanaged long."

Emerson now turns to the notion of the microcosm. "The world globes itself in a drop of dew." Since "Every thing in nature contains all the powers of nature," it follows that the world-wide law of equilibration operates in each little world. "The dice of God are always loaded. The world looks like a multiplication-table, or a mathematical equation, which, turn it how you will, balances itself. Take what figure you will, its exact value, nor more nor less, still returns to you." Then the specific moral statement: "Every secret is told, every crime is punished, each virtue rewarded, every wrong redressed, in silence and certainty." Soon Emerson repeats himself, memorably if with unsupported optimism: "Crime and punishment grow out of one stem." Each act in its very nature carries its own consequences. Only the sensualist refuses to admit this: "he sees the mermaid's head but not the dragon's tail . . ."

Innumerable fables and proverbs show all of this to be true. Tithonus was given immortality all right, but he grew impossibly old. Achilles and Siegfried proved vulnerable. Imperfection in this world is inevitable. "There is a crack in every thing God has made." This is so because "in nature nothing can be given, all things are sold." As for proverbs, we have long heard about tit for tat; an eye for an eye; nothing venture, nothing have; etc. "It is thus written, because it is thus in life." This being the case, what should we do? Pay every debt with religious scrupulosity, dread unearned prosperity, realize that there are no shortcuts to any goal but only a laborious road to it. Emerson goes so far as to add a little later, "I no longer wish to meet a good I do not earn, for example to find a pot of buried gold, knowing that it brings with it new burdens."

As though aware that many of his readers might be chafing restlessly at about this point, Emerson now turns to two related questions. What good can come of suffering and weakness? And can vice produce good out of itself? Emerson forcefully argues that faults, injuries, wounds, weaknesses, criticism, and bloody persecutions are all reversed by a compensatory deity. "Put God in your debt. Every stroke shall be repaid." We should thank our faults. Injuries only strengthen us; remember that "the wounded oyster . . . mends his shell with pearl." Therefore "Blame is safer than praise"; also "The martyr cannot be dishonored. Every lash is a tongue of fame; every prison a more illustrious abode; every burned book or house enlightens the world; every suppressed or expunged word reverberates through the earth from side to side." Becoming personal although naming no names, Emerson considers the mentally defective, whose afflictions seem terribly unjust. But "Love reduces them as the sun melts the iceberg in the sea. The heart and soul of all men being one, this bitterness of *His* and *Mine* ceases. His is mine. I am my brother and my brother is me. . . . His virtue,—is not that mine? His wit,—if it cannot be made mine, it is not wit." (Surely Emerson was thinking of his mentally retarded brother Bulkeley at this point.)

Those who feel like lapsing into indifference on the grounds that good will inevitably come out of vice, falsehood, and the powers of darkness, Emerson lectures as follows: "Nothing, Falsehood, may indeed stand as the great Night or shade on which as a background the living universe paints itself forth, but no fact is begotten by it; it cannot work, for it is not. It cannot work any good; it cannot work any harm. It is harm inasmuch as it is worse not to be than to be." In other words, lies and other negatives can produce nothing positive because they are utterly sterile and void. On the other hand, one should not fear good on the specious grounds that good must be purchased at the expense of another good. "There is no penalty to virtue; no penalty to wisdom; they

are proper additions of being." One can add to beauty, goodness, and truth without taking away from something else.

With romantic stoicism Emerson concludes by contending
that apparent losses, even the most dreadful, are compensated
for by a concomitant maturing in the survivor: ". . . the
compensations of calamity are made apparent to the understanding also, after long intervals of time. A fever, a mutila-
tion, a cruel disappointment, a loss of wealth, a loss of friends,
seems at the moment unpaid loss, and unpayable. But the
sure years reveal the deep remedial force that underlies all
facts. The death of a dear friend, wife, brother, lover, which
seemed nothing but privation, somewhat later assumes the
aspect of a guide or genius . . ." This is so because such an
event ends a phase of dependence which needed ending and
permits independent growth in the survivor, so that he in turn
can guide those who have not yet suffered loss.

The Over-Soul

Like "Self-Reliance" and "Compensation," "The Over-
Soul" was published in *Essays, First Series,* in 1841. It complements the other two essays and thus illustrates the law of
compensation in Emerson's own eclectic philosophy. Whereas
"Self-Reliance" stems from the earlier "American Scholar"
in espousing rugged individualism, "The Over-Soul" seems
to derive from the idealism of the even earlier "Nature." *

"The Over-Soul" is a controversial essay. Those who like
mysticism revere it, and tough-minded modern realists dislike
it; but most readers if they are mature can appreciate its
artistry whether they accept its message or not. Everyone can

---

* Unless otherwise stated, by "Nature" is meant Emerson's short 1836
book and not the essay of the same title which is part of *Essays, Second
Series,* 1844.

point out passages in it which are partly incomprehensible. But the master metaphor of the whole essay is highly important to an understanding of Emerson the Transcendentalist, to whom the Over-Soul is a vast beatific field of spiritual power to which our individual souls platonically connect if we let them.

Emerson opens his argument with a fine rhetorical question: "We grant that human life is mean, but how did we find out that it was mean?" The answer? "Man is a stream whose source is hidden. Our being is descending into us from we know not whence." Our habitually vicious lives obscure the source, but in brief moments we have valuable intuitions concerning it; and it is "that Unity, that Over-Soul, within which every man's particular being is contained and made one with all other . . ." Not only is the individual life splintered into divisions and particles, but so is the universe into sun, beast, plant, and stone; however, "the whole, of which these [fractions] are the shining parts, is the soul." Even though the soul is ineffable, one can report hints as to its essence. The image to use in suggesting it is the age-old one of light. "From within or from behind, a light shines through us upon things and makes us aware that we are nothing, but the light is all." When this light illuminates the intellect, we have genius; will, virtue; affections, love. We can profit by this infusion not by trying to control it but only when we "let it have its way through us." The supremacy of the Over-Soul is attested to by its effortless ability to abolish time, space, and nature. We worry about youth and age, distance, and physical objects, but only until the soul renders us indifferent to such things and activates our "love of the universal and eternal beauty." Gradually we realize that spiritual growth is distinct from time, as is mental growth. There is a difference, however, between the two: whereas "our ordinary education often labors to silence and obstruct" ordinary persons in their efforts to rise to the level of the wisest people on earth, spiritual energy always strives to unite all souls. "We owe many valuable observations to people who are not very acute or profound, and who say the thing without effort which we want and have long been hunting in vain." This is so because all people have their share in the Supreme Mind. Still, ordinary social meetings are a disappontment—"Men descend to meet"—because they rarely display their genuine spiritual riches to each other.

"The soul is the perceiver and revealer of truth." We naturally recognize the truth when we see it, in good thoughts coming to us from books, in revelations flowing into us from God's world all about. This inflowing awareness is sometimes only a faint glow, but at other times is "an ecstasy and trance and prophetic inspiration." Whatever its intensity, the experience is mystical when "the individual soul . . . mingles with the universal soul." One mistake which some sharers of this "awe and delight" make is to ask the soul to make revelations. "But we must pick no locks. We must check this low curiosity." It is sinful to ask the soul to tell us about the future life, which we will know about once we get there: "Do not require a description of the countries towards which you sail. The description does not describe them to you, and to-morrow you arrive there and know them by inhabiting them." Though the soul knows, it cannot reduce the ineffable to patois.

Similarly, it is useless to ask a philosopher or anyone else to explain reality to you. Two classes of people often try. One group is merely "accomplished talkers," who try to explain from without, and who talk like spectators or persons who have second-hand evidence. The other group is the "fervent mystic[s]"; they wisely speak from within. Emerson says impatiently: "It is of no use to preach to me from without. I can do that too easily myself. Jesus speaks always from within, and in a degree that transcends all others. In that is the miracle. I believe beforehand that it ought so to be." Thus the real philosopher teaches by reminding us of what we already know; he evokes what is already within us. More than this, the truly great writer makes us feel that what he has written— his amazingly clear revelation of the truth—has somehow already existed in us. He speaks from within, and curiously we therefore value his works less. "The great poet makes us feel our own wealth, and then we think less of his compositions."

The wisdom of such an artist is superior to his mere talent, which is God-given. Therefore, unlike the "ambitious vulgar" and the slightly more "cultivated" who boast and drop names and show material proofs of their experiences, "the soul that ascends to worship the great God is plain and true."

Awareness that the brooding Over-Soul is pervasive should make us indifferent to even the grandest literature. "The simplest utterances are worthiest to be written, yet are they so cheap and so things of course, that in the infinite riches of the soul it is like gathering a few pebbles off the ground, or bottling a little air in a phial, when the whole earth and the whole atmosphere are ours." When persons who realize this talk with us, their "sincerity is more excellent than flattery." They know, and we should too, that "The simplest person who in his integrity worships God, becomes God." And the one who is sure of his God—who knows that he is part of the Over-Soul—is inevitably sure of himself. In two concluding paragraphs, Emerson invites everyone to realize that "the Highest dwells with him" and that "the sources of nature are in his own mind." (This is reminiscent of the last three sections of "Nature.") Therefore everyone "must listen greatly to himself." (This sounds like "Self-Reliance" again.) No belief can be validated by statistics. Each individual soul must go it alone: "The soul gives itself, alone, original, and pure, to the Lonely, Original, and Pure." When each person knows this and allows himself to be "born into the great, the universal mind," all of reality will flower into "the perennial miracle."

The Poet

"The Poet" is the first item in *Essays, Second Series,* 1844, which also includes "Experience," "Politics," and "New England Reformers." The essays in this series are generally notable for more realistic and less poetic treatment of somewhat more practical subjects.

"The Poet" is Emerson's most significant and frequently reprinted essay on aesthetics. Because of its appeal to modern psychologists and literary critics, it is growing even more popular. It is unusually well organized. It begins by describing the ideal poet and his relations to other people. It continues by distinguishing between those valuable elements in nature which stir the poet and give him his symbols, and those frothy elements which merely tease his fancy. Then it concludes by criticizing contemporary poetry for mere prettiness and by challenging the nation to produce a really splendid poet who will take our realities into consideration. In relating to the sections called "Beauty" and "Language" in the long essay "Nature," this essay harks back to familiar old Emersonian Platonism, but its practical ending, like the conclusion of "The American Scholar," is forward-looking. Many of the main points of the essay are taken up symbolically in several of Emerson's poems, for example, "Merlin," "Bacchus," "Saadi," and "The Poet."

Emerson begins by portraying the ideal poet. He is a

complete man, complete because he is in tune with his times and also because he can express those times. He is not selfish, sensual, or petty. Too many so-called poets "are contented with a civil and conformed manner of living, and to write poems from the fancy, at a safe distance from their own experience." Not so the genuine "sayer," who because of his special vision "is isolated among his contemporaries by truth and by his art, but with this consolation in his pursuits, that they will draw all men sooner or later." One can prove that expressive poets are rare by noting that it is seldom enough that the average person can even report in conversation what has happened to him.

Emerson now places the poet in a trinity which also includes the knower and the doer. The knower loves the truth; the doer, good; and the poet or "sayer," beauty. And "each of these three has the power of the others latent in him and his own, patent." Thus, the ideal poet is potentially a knower of truth and a doer of good as well as actually a singer of beauty. All poetry has existed before the beginning of time and is simply waiting to be expressed. Hence the true poet, unlike the poetaster, is not simply a contemporary but "an eternal man."

Emerson suddenly advances the theory of the organic quality of poetry with these deservedly famous lines: "For it is not metres, but a metre-making argument that makes a poem,—a thought so passionate and alive that like the spirit of a plant or an animal it has an architecture of its own, and adorns nature with a new thing." Such a vital thought when it grows into poetic reality adds to the living world and helps tell us the secret of all things. Ordinary men impatiently await the advent of a poet having such vision and with it the power of expression; "but the fruition is postponed. Oftener it falls that this winged man, who will carry me into the heavens, whirls me into mists, then leaps and frisks about . . . ; but the all-piercing, all-feeding and ocular air of heaven that man shall never inhabit."

The main body of the essay follows, and in it Emerson points out the elements in nature which the poet can weave into poetic symbols. "Things admit of being used as symbols because nature is a symbol, in the whole, and in every part." The average person may not realize this—and hence he may think that he dislikes poetry—but the truth is that everything tangible is "the externalization of the soul." Therefore "there is no fact in nature which does not carry the whole sense of nature." So the specific make-up of a given experience is of no real significance, and the would-be poet is wrong to complain that he needs more materials, more experiences, to work with before he can write. "Why covet a knowledge of new facts? Day and night, house and garden, a few books, a few actions, serve us as well as would all trades and all spectacles."

Emerson next anticipates his concluding call for the American poet by suddenly interpolating this prediction that the poet will soon use modern artifacts as poetic symbols: "Readers of poetry see the factory-village and the railway, and fancy that the poetry of the landscape is broken up by these; for these works of art are not yet consecrated in their reading; but the poet sees them fall within the great Order not less than the beehive or the spider's geometrical web. Nature adopts them very fast into her vital circles, and the gliding trains of cars she loves like her own." (Here Emerson seems to predict aspects of the work of Walt Whitman, Emily Dickinson, and Hart Crane, among many others.) The poet is simply the one who observes reality, revels in language— which is "fossil poetry"—articulates his inner and outer vision, and scatters the resulting verse like seeds.

Next Emerson considers the poetic process. First inspiration, then imagination. The poet must be genuinely inspired, by some beauty in nature which his ready eye reflects. Some stimulants—"wine, mead, narcotics, . . . or whatever"—may help; but "spurious mode[s]" frustrate by deteriorating and jading the true poet, who "should be tipsy with water." Then comes the attempt at organic expression. Since the resulting "poems are a corrupt version of some text in nature with which they ought to be made to tally," the critic has the one legitimate function here of trying to show wherein the expression may not "tally." Because all persons are intoxicated by the ever-liberating imagination, the poet is special only in degree. We all have the trope-making faculty, although poetic genius has the ability in a greater amount. But all people are capable of being elevated by seeing the imagination transform natural objects into poetic symbols. "The use of symbols has a certain power of emancipation and exhilaration for all men. We seem to be touched by a wand which makes us dance and run about happily, like children. We are like persons who come out of a cave or cellar into the open air. This is the effect on us of tropes, fables, oracles and all poetic forms." Thus "the poets are . . . liberating gods," but the combination of nature and anyone's imagination is liberating. We insufficiently prize this liberation, the means of which are close to hand. "The fate of the poor shepherd, who, blinded and lost in the snow-storm, perishes in a drift within a few feet of his cottage door, is an emblem of the state of man. On the brink of the waters of life and truth, we are miserably dying."

Toward the end, Emerson valuably contrasts mystics and poets, both of whom are imaginative and hence liberating. But "the difference betwixt the poet and the mystic . . . [is] that the last nails a symbol to one sense, which was a true sense for a moment, but soon becomes old and false." Distinguishing here between old-fashioned allegory and modern symbolism, Emerson is again forward-looking.

Finally Emerson tersely criticizes the practicing poets of his day. "I look in vain for the poet whom I describe." We have marvelous raw material for poetry in America, he insists, but it is not yet used. "Our log-rolling, our stumps and their politics, our fisheries, our Negroes and Indians, our boats and our repudiations, the wrath of rogues and the pusillanimity of honest men, the northern trade, the southern planting, the western clearing, Oregon and Texas, are yet unsung. Yet America is a poem in our eyes; its ample geography dazzles the imagination, and it will not wait long for metres." (This chant sounds for all the world like a prediction of the coming soon of *The Oregon Trail,* Whittier's *Songs of Labor, Walden, Hiawatha, Leaves of Grass,* some of Bret Harte's local-color stories, and even *Roughing It, Life on the Mississippi,* and *Huckleberry Finn.* Emerson would be the last to insist that poetic America should be expressed only in poetry and not also in poetic prose.)

Emerson closes by challenging the true poet to be inspired by what he sees near at hand, exercise his imagination upon it, and be surprised by the resulting expression. He should "resemble a mirror carried through the street, ready to render an image of every created thing." He should let a poetic "rage draw out of [him] that *dream*-power which every night shows [him] is [his] own." His reward will be that "the ideal shall be real to [him]," and whereas lesser persons are only "tenants and boarders" in nature, he will own the land, sea, and woods.

Experience

Infrequently anthologized in the past, the startling essay "Experience" is gaining with modern editors and readers because it boldly reflects the more and more popular pragmatic side of its author. Early critics disliked "Experience" for apparently rambling, but more recent commentators have emphasized the fact that it moves from negative to positive, from confusion to resolution, from actual to ideal. It begins by pointing out the seeming puzzles and paradoxes and confusing bemuddlements of life, and it ends by challenging us to do with life what incidentally we must do with Emerson's essays—piece together conflicting bits into a stable and meaningful whole.

Emerson boldly begins by imaging man as on a stairway, which has steps below and steps above; and "All things swim and glitter." In such a dismaying confusion, "All our days are unprofitable" and "life looks trivial." Mere preparation, routine, and inefficient looking back sour our days. We are so bored that we even "court suffering, in the hope that here at least we shall find reality, sharp peaks and edges of truth." But grief teaches only that grief is shallow. Emerson then becomes personal and writes of the death of his son Waldo (which event was perhaps the motivating force behind the essay): "In the death of my son, now more than two years ago, I seem to have lost a beautiful estate,—no more. . . . I grieve that grief can teach me nothing." (This passage has been misunderstood out of context and gives a false picture of Emerson as cold.)

"Life is a train of moods like a string of beads, and as we pass through them they prove to be many-colored lenses which paint the world their own hue, and each shows only what lies in its focus." We are often in such a mood as not to relish the beauties of nature or the ostensibly helpful comments of friends. And some people are of such a temperament that the best sunset or the most positive criticism is lost on them. Scientists are coming along and trying to explain in materialistic terms the most spiritual of verities, and the attempt takes the mystery out of such things as love and religion. "I had fancied [Emerson adds] that the value of life lay in its inscrutable possibilities." But science wants to truncate man and explain away everything about him as the result of natural forces. "I see not, if one be once caught in this trap of so-called sciences, any escape for the man from the links of the chain of physical necessity." (Thus Emerson inveighs against the implications of philosophical naturalism almost half a century before it became popular in American thought.)

Gradually Emerson's mood changes from deep bitterness, frustration, and melancholy to guarded hope. Life seems illusory, but this is because we necessarily lack the power to concentrate on one truth for very long. Such concentration would be harmful, just as lack of circulation hurts bodily health and lack of variety hurts mental health. The apparent lack of significance in daily events and the seeming inability of friends to achieve our notion of their potential screen from us the fact that in little ways we gain wisdom from all events and all friends. Apparent folly and defect are a part of the vast scheme of things, but we can see this only from a kind of cosmic perspective. "The party-colored wheel must revolve very fast to appear white. . . . The plays of children are non-sense, but very educative nonsense. So it is with the largest and solemnest things."

The best way one can manage his life in such a confusing world is to keep busy. "Intellectual tasting of life will not supersede muscular activity." And then, "Do not craze yourself with thinking, but go about your business anywhere. Life is not intellectual or critical, but sturdy. Its chief good is for well-mixed people who can enjoy what they find, without question. . . . To fill the hour,—that is happiness . . ." Instead of moaning about unrealized potential and attractive alternatives, keep busy, be "thankful for small mercies," expect nothing, and you will "have heaping measures." While hair-splitting disputes continue endlessly, "stick to thy foolish task, add a line every hour, and between times add a line. . . . dig away in your garden . . . stay there in thy closet and toil . . . finish that stint."

If we work in this fashion, we may not see much progress daily, "But ah! presently comes a day, or is it only a half-hour, with its angel-whispering . . ." Power will flow into us by "the subterranean and invisible tunnels and channels of life." Instead of placing faith in mere chance, we will suddenly be surprised by the realization that the miraculous but predictable process of synthesis has been going on. "Bear with these distractions, with this coetaneous growth of the parts; they will one day be *members,* and obey one will." Then we will agree that, in spite of the evident "flux of moods, . . . there is that in us which changes not and which ranks all sensations and states of mind."

Emerson begins his conclusion with this startling comment: "It is very unhappy, but too late to be helped, the discovery we have made that we exist. That discovery is called the Fall of Man." We must accept the inevitable coloring and distorting by our "subject-lenses" of whatever is out there in outer nature. We must also accept "the same gulf between every me and thee as between the original and the picture." Each of us believes in himself. "We permit all things to ourselves, and that which we call sin in others is experiment for us." Others feel the same way. So morals seem to be relative. Inevitably each of us colors his notion of reality, and reality needs each of us to color it. "A subject and an object,—it takes so much to make the galvanic circuit complete, but magnitude adds nothing." The stars need their Kepler, America its Columbus, and the chased tail its kitten. One should be him-

self, hold to these hard and even mournful truths, and do less
mouthing about them.

Emerson ends this remarkably frank and provocative
essay thus:

> Illusion, Temperament, Succession, Surface, Surprise,
> Reality, Subjectiveness,—these are threads on the loom
> of time, these are the lords of life. I dare not assume to
> give their order, but I name them as I find them in my
> way. I know better than to claim any completeness for
> my picture. I am a fragment, and this is a fragment of
> me. I can confidently announce one or another law,
> which throws itself into [temporary] relief and form,
> but I am too young yet by some ages to compile a code.
> I gossip for my hour concerning the eternal politics.
> . . . Let who will ask, Where is the fruit? I find a
> private fruit sufficient. This is a fruit,—that I should not
> ask for a rash effect from meditations . . .

We should be thankful for experience. We should seek no
immediate practical good from it. We should work away; if
we do, what hope we entertain will be fulfilled. "Never mind
the ridicule, never mind the defeat; up again, old heart!"

Politics

Emerson's essay "Politics" is rarely reprinted now. It so
neatly balances hope and fear, individualism and respect for
the other side, and awareness of the validity of both law for
man and law for thing that it will probably always be provocative if bewildering in spots. It grew out of several lectures and
much thought over many years—years marked for Emerson
by juvenile conservatism in Whiggish Boston, disgust with the
crudities of Jacksonian democracy, and the espousal of Trans-

cendental liberalism. Like those of "Nature," its parts required soldering or welding. The tone is academic, almost Olympian; therefore it frustrated contemporary partisans looking for support. For example, midway through "Politics" Emerson pontificates thus:

> Of the two great parties [Democratic and Whig] which at this hour [1844] almost share the nation between them, I should say that one [Democratic] has the best cause, and the other [Whig] contains the best men [Daniel Webster, Henry Clay, Charles Francis Adams]. The philosopher, the poet, or the religious man, will of course wish to cast his vote with the democrat, for free-trade, for wide suffrage, for the abolition of legal cruel-ties in the penal code, and for facilitating in every man-ner the access of the young and the poor to the sources of wealth and power. But he can rarely accept the per-sons whom the so-called popular party propose to him as representatives of these liberalities. The spirit of our American radicalism is destructive and aimless . . . On the other side, the conservative party, composed of the most moderate, able and cultivated part of the popu-lation, is timid, and merely defensive of property. . . . From neither party, when in power, has the world any benefit to expect . . . at all commensurate with the re-sources of the nation.

In the first third of the essay Emerson discusses the two foundations of most present-day political institutions—respect for the individual and respect for property. "The theory of politics . . . considers persons and property as the two objects for whose protection government exists." Being "identical in nature," all people have equal personal rights; however, since "One man owns [only] his clothes, and another owns a county"—because skill, virtue, and inheritances differ—property rights are unequal. Recently, many thinkers have concluded that property laws have unjustly aided the rich and held down the poor, further, that "the only interest for the consideration of the State is persons . . ." But Emerson rather loftily adds that "Things have their laws, as well as men; and things refuse to be trifled with. Property will be protected." (This does not sound much like the author of the "Channing Ode.") Men will work hard to produce things only if they have a reasonable guarantee that they can reap the benefit of their labor. Therefore, ultimately, "by a higher law, the property will, year after year, write every statute that respects property." What the sweat of man produces has a value which must be respected.

Next Emerson gets into the subject of the relative value of unlike political institutions. Each nation naturally evolves its own particular form of government, "from the character and condition of the people." As for our own governmental institutions, "They are not better, but only fitter for us." And so we are wrong to be vain concerning them and are presumptuous if we judge the monarchical system, for example, as inferior. Unfortunately every system is weakened by personality, opportunism, and enthusiasm. "Every actual State is corrupt." This is so because leaders usually act through force of circumstance rather than by principle. But this natural situation should not cause despair, since "In the strife of ferocious parties, human nature always finds itself cherished; as the children of the convicts in Botany Bay are found to have as healthy a moral sentiment as other children." Critics of the American system feel that "in our license of construing the Constitution, and in the despotism of public opinion, we have no anchor." But Emerson finds great cause for faith in "the laws of things," that is, the law that for every force in political action there is compensatory opposing force. "The fact of two poles, of two forces, centripetal and centrifugal, is universal . . . Wild liberty develops iron conscience." Mob action instantly causes mob reaction, "and only justice satisfies all." The end of all government, in spite of temporary miseries to the contrary, is the application of truth and justice to the protection of human rights and property rights.

In the last third of "Politics" Emerson considers the anarchistic thesis that "The wise man is the State." The purpose of the state is to educate the wise man, who "needs no army, fort, or navy,—he loves men too well; no bribe, or feast, or palace, to draw friends to him; no vantage ground, no favorable circumstance. He needs no library, for he has not done thinking; no church, for he is a prophet; no statute-book, for he has the lawgiver; no money, for he is value; no road, for he is at home where he is; no experience, for the life of the creator shoots through him, and looks from his eyes." When every individual is thus well educated, government will be unnecessary; ". . . the less government we have the better,—the fewer laws, and the less confided power." We wrongly think that "our civilization [is] near its meridian, but we are yet only at the cock-crowing and the morning star." We excessively praise success in trade because we sense lack of it in politics. Modern times have been marked by a general tendency of revolt toward more and more self-government. "It promises a recognition of higher rights than those of personal freedom, or the security of property. A man has a right to be employed, to be trusted, to be loved, to be revered." Perhaps the next step is to try a form of government based entirely on love and moral sentiment rather than force; ". . . nature continue[s] to fill the heart of youth with suggestions of this enthusiasm."

New England Reformers

This delightful essay is undeservedly neglected. In it Emerson delicately balances himself between criticism of half-baked reformers and sympathy for the sincerity of other reformers, between idealistic hope for the success of certain reforms and canny awareness that most reform has little chance of lasting success. The essay itself has two tones, an engaging humor at first and then sincere shrewdness.

Emerson opens "New England Reformers" with a humorous attack on the excesses of many reforms. "What a fertility of projects for the salvation of the world! One apostle thought all men should go to farming, and another that no man should buy or sell, that the use of money was the cardinal evil; another that the mischief was in our diet, that we eat and drink damnation. These made unleavened bread, and were foes to the death to fermentation." And so on and on. But behind "this din of opinion and debate" two valuable trends may be noted, an advocacy of simpler methods and praise of individualism.

Next Emerson goes over the various fields in which reformational zeal is now being practiced: politics, civil and domestic society, and education. He takes a side-track into the realm of classical *vs.* vocational education, asserting at some length that since the aim of reform is "to cast aside the superfluous and arrive at short methods," the study of Greek, Latin, and even mathematics should be reserved for those who genuinely love those subjects and not required for, say, those going into law, medicine, and practical religion. "Four, or six, or ten years, the pupil is parsing Greek and Latin, and as soon as he leaves the University, as it is ludicrously styled, he shuts those books for the last time." Require only those men to learn the ancient languages who are drawn to their "great beauty of structure, . . . [and their] wonderful remains of genius."

Before getting into the idealistic heart of his essay, Emerson feels obliged to rebuke hypocritical, short-sighted, partial reformers. "Do you complain of our Marriage? Our marriage is no worse than our education, our diet, our trade, our social customs." Such one-track minds should realize that "the new and renewing principle of love" would help their pet projects and much else. Emerson also criticizes would-be reformers who rely on the power of concerted action, on unions or associations of their fellows. Although such projects as those of Fourier and Owen arouse much interest, they are falsely based on defeatism—"I have failed, and you have failed, but perhaps together we shall not fail"—and aim to create a retreat, an asylum, rather than "a field to the strong." Emerson closes this section by saying cryptically that "The union must be ideal in actual individualism," that is, concerted action toward one goal is most efficient when each member is free to advance the interests of his group when he feels like it and in his own manner.

Now Emerson advances his main point. To be effective, reform cannot develop from any lack of faith in the potentialities of human beings but rather from the honest, self-reliant individual's efforts to realize his own potential. It is utter "infidelity" in us, but the truth is that "We believe that the defects of so many perverse and so many frivolous people who make up society, are organic, and society is a hospital of incurables." Further, we lack faith "that any education, any system of philosophy, any influence of genius, will ever give depth of insight to a superficial mind." Worst of all, some supposedly good and wise writers doubt whether "the happiness and probity of men is increased by the culture of the mind in those disciplines to which we give the name of education." Instead, Emerson argues persuasively but at too much length that we must fight all skepticism, believe that observable differences in people are not organic and necessarily divisive—"every man has at intervals the grace to scorn his performances, in comparing them with his belief of what he should do"—and take criticism for what it is, a challenge to see reality more steadily even if it causes pain, and a challenge constantly to improve ourselves. In turn, perhaps we criticize reformers in order to make them see all of reality more clearly and to "hear ourselves confuted" by their responses.

Emerson absolutely denies the modern theory that man is depraved and nature is malign: "the general purpose in the great number of persons is fidelity," and one man is the equal of a whole church, a whole state, and even every other man. A poet may feel superior to inarticulate men, but all he has in addition to the same manhood they have is the "knack" of expression. We should realize that "There is power over and behind us, and we are the channels of its communication"; we should give in to the "traitor" within us who seeks to bring us to "the highest life," in which "Men are all secret believers . . . , else the word justice would have no meaning: they believe that the best is true; that right is done at last; or chaos would come." If each man would simply work hard, whether "planting corn or writing epics," he would stop all of this partial and concerted criticism "of this or that teacher or experimenter"—soon enough they will see their own deficiencies—and then all of us would realize that "our own orbit is all our task, and we need not assist the administration of the universe."

Every man should be cheerful and courageous, and work hard to realize his own aspirations.

Plato; or, the Philosopher

Emerson's essays on Plato, the representative philosopher, and Montaigne, the typical skeptic, are more often reprinted than any of the other essays which with "Plato" and "Montaigne" comprise *Representative Men* (1850). The other chapters are as follows: "Uses of Great Men," "Swedenborg; or, the Mystic," "Shakespeare; or, the Poet," "Napoleon; or, the Man of the World," and "Goethe; or, the Writer."

Plato was always a great influence upon Emerson, because of his theory of the union of opposites, his idealistic conception of nature, his stress on the Transcendental importance of mind over matter and events, and his attitudes toward art. But Platonism and neo-Platonism often so closely resemble two other philosophical delights of Emerson—Oriental mysticism and German idealism—that Plato's influence upon Emerson is difficult to trace.

Emerson begins by exalting Plato as a writer of staggering influence. "Out of Plato come all things that are still written and debated among men of thought." He is behind a long list of writers; moreover, Christianity, Mohammedanism, Calvinism, and mysticism find support in his works. Plato made complete use of his own times, absorbed all available learning, and in addition traveled. "This breadth entitles him to stand as the representative of philosophy." As with all great geniuses, we know little about his life. "If he had lover, wife, or children, we hear nothing of them. He ground them all into paint. As a good chimney burns its smoke, so a philosopher converts the value of all his fortunes into his intellectual performances." Only his inner life is of consequence.

That said, Emerson becomes highly abstract. He says that Plato in honoring both the ideal (the laws of the mind) and fate (the order of nature) was a dualist, while in trying to see unity (or identity) behind or above variety Plato was a monist. The East has tended to philosophize on unity. Emerson quotes from a Hindu scripture: "What is the great end of all, you shall now learn from me. It is soul,—one in all bodies . . ." Meanwhile, the West illustrates disunity, as Emerson goes on to point out: "If speculation tends . . . to a terrific unity, in which all things are absorbed, action tends directly backwards to diversity." Every student leans toward unifying speculation or divisive observation and experimentation. And so it is with nations too: "The country of unity . . . is Asia" (Emerson nicknamed his wife Lidian "Mine Asia"), whereas the countries of "the West delighted in boundaries." Along came Plato, "to join, and, by contact, to enhance the energy of each. The excellence of Europe and Asia are in his brain." Plato can see both sides of the medal of Jove. Like all artists, he is a synthesis, a combination of high imagination and homely common sense, of boldness and discretion, who uses every "weapon in all the armory of wit." (In thus praising Plato, Emerson would seem to be mostly describing himself —or rather the sort of writer he aspired to be, that is, a combination of mystic and pragmatist.)

The last half of "Plato" is a curious mixture. Emerson attempts to summarize Plato's message poetically and abstractly; then he gives a charmingly down-to-earth, homely sketch of Plato's idol, Socrates; and finally Emerson briefly criticizes Plato and then concludes with words of enormous praise, just as he began.

Emerson points out that Plato, while admitting that ultimate truths are beyond the limits of the human intellect and are literally ineffable, believes that they are nonetheless knowable through correspondences: "being from one, things correspond. There is a scale; and the correspondence of heaven to earth, of matter to mind, of the part to the whole, is our guide. . . . there is a science of sciences,—I call it Dialectic, —which is the Intellect discriminating the false and the true. It rests on the observation of identity and diversity; for to judge is to unite to an object the notion which belongs to it." As for the scale or ladder, all things want to move up it from natural diversity to divine unity. (Note Emerson's poem "Initial, Dæmonic, and Celestial Love.") "As every pool reflects the image of the sun, so every thought and thing restores us an image and creature of the supreme Good. The universe is perforated by a million channels for his activity. All things mount and mount," from petty activity, through awareness of beauty, to achievement of wisdom. Plato knows that his vision and his methods are difficult, and he realistically recognizes that "the generality of men" can never be taught all "orders of things." Emerson shows the method to be difficult indeed by giving a confusing explication of Plato's curious figure of the twice-bisected line. Cut a line into two unequal parts, and then cut each part again. One original part represents the visible world; its halves, the unclear (shadows and reflections of real things) and the clear (the real things seen— plants, animals, art works, nature, etc.). The other original part represents the world of the intelligence; its halves, the unclear (opinions and hypotheses) and the clear (truth). Reflections of reality and reality itself stand in the visible world in the same relation to each other as conjecture and faith do in the world of intelligence. (Emerson goes on to imply that the understanding works with "shadows and reflections" and "conjectures"—in the realm of the "dark"—whereas the reason works with "truth," in the realm of the "bright." It has been pointed out by Professors Walter Blair and Clarence Faust [see the Bibliography] that Emerson's literary method in many essays and poems is to move from illusion and hypothesis to reason and truth—that is, from actual to ideal—or vice versa. Hence, the twice-bisected line symbolizes Emerson's literary method.)

As though to come back down to common reality again, Emerson next gives a pithy character sketch of Socrates. He was good humored, sweet tempered, attracted to drink, dreadfully logical, pitiless in debate, humorously hypocritical in pretending to know nothing, and relentlessly honest and just. Emerson makes him into almost a village personality, "Plain old uncle as he was, with his great ears . . ." Socrates inspired Plato, the "robed scholar": "The rare coincidence, in one ugly body, of the droll and the martyr, the keen street and market debater with the sweetest saint known to any history at that time, had forcibly struck the mind of Plato, so capacious of these contrasts . . ." And as for Socrates's inspiring death— "The fame of this prison, the fame of these discourses there and the drinking of the hemlock are one of the most precious passages in the history of the world." Like Socrates, like Plato, like Emerson's personality and philosophy, Emerson's character sketch of Socrates has reflections and reality, hypotheses and high truth.

Finally, Emerson briefly criticizes Plato and then ends with more praise. Plato is "literary" (like Emerson), and therefore his message lacks "the vital authority which the screams of prophets and the sermons of unlettered Arabs and Jews possess. There is an interval; and to cohesion, contact is necessary." Also Plato (again like Emerson) has no system. Concerning everything in the universe, "his theory is not complete or self-evident." Further, "He is charged with having failed to make the transition from ideas to matter." (Emerson knew that the reverse was true of his own essay "Nature.") Like a boa constrictor trying to swallow too much and hence failing, Plato unsuccessfully sought to embrace the whole world—"this mammoth morsel . . . There he perishes: unconquered nature lives on and forgets him." Emerson, however, cannot end thus negatively. He must add this tremendous praise:

> But there is an injustice in assuming this ambition for Plato. Let us not seem to treat with flippancy his venerable name. Men, in proportion to their intellect, have admitted his transcendent claims. The way to know him is to compare him, not with nature, but with other men. How many ages have gone by, and he remains unapproached! A chief structure of human wit, like Karnac, or the mediaeval cathedrals, or the Etrurian remains, it requires all the breadth of human faculty to know it. I think it is trueliest seen when seen with the most respect.

Montaigne; or, the Skeptic

Emerson's vigorous essay on Montaigne, whose philosophy is less in accord with Emerson's own than Plato's is, has proved to be more popular than the essay on Plato. Short and far less abstract, "Montaigne" appeals to modern readers because, like the essay "Experience," it helps to counter the traditional and false stereotype of Emerson as a soft optimist and an unquestioning idealist. "Montaigne" should be seen as the obverse of "Nature" and "The American Scholar." Even while Emerson gives the skeptic Montaigne his day in court —more than that, he joyously lauds the man's withering honesty—he is rejecting the posture of the skeptic as anything more than temporary. Man must believe; through belief, muted and darkened though it necessarily is by temporal experience, he gains serenity and with Plato ascends the ladder to the unfading ideals.

This logical essay is in four parts. First Emerson provides

the rationale behind skepticism. Then he briefly explains his love for Montaigne and Montaigne's intellectual traits. Next Emerson presents the average skeptic's major premises. And finally he answers the skeptic by espousing idealism and faith in the moral sentiment.

Emerson begins by explaining that the coin of reality has two sides: "This head and this tail are called, in the language of philosophy, Infinite and Finite; Relative and Absolute; Apparent and Real; and many fine names beside." Most of us arrogantly prefer one side or the other, and are intolerant of those who disagree with us. Thus, the genius, contemplating the ideal, is disappointed by mere reality; on the other hand practical merchants and politicians call thinkers fools. Enter the skeptic. "The abstractionist and the materialist thus mutually exasperating each other, . . . there arises a third party to occupy the middle ground between these two, the skeptic, namely. He finds both wrong by being in extremes." His message is this: "What is the use of pretending to assurances we have not, respecting the other life? Why exaggerate the power of virtue? Why be an angel before your time? These strings, wound up too high, will snap. If there is a wish for immortality, and no evidence, why not say just that? If there are conflicting evidences, why not state them?" And so on. The skeptic has many areas for honest doubt—such as marriage, government, religion, labor, and education. Seeing man as a "little conceited vulnerable popinjay," the skeptic naturally wants a flexible philosophy—neither too stiff (like that of Spartans and Stoics) nor too soft (like that of St. John). He wants to go through life adaptively, like a trim ship which can ride the billows, not "An angular, dogmatic house [which] would be rent to chips and splinters in this storm of many elements." Emerson then leads into his consideration of Montaigne specifically, by adding that the only admissible kind of skeptic, the only one entitled to "fellow-ship and trust" amid idealists and materialists alike is the skeptic who can prove that he has played the game of life "with skill and success"; "boys, coxcombs, and pedants" who profess skepticism without being tried by life cannot qualify as solid and intelligent skeptics.

Emerson begins his brief sketch of Montaigne by report-ing that only after college did he read Charles Cotton's trans-lation of Montaigne's *Essays* in a copy his father owned, that he saw a tomb in Paris in 1833 marked to the effect that the man buried there "had formed himself to virtue on the Es-says of Montaigne," that John Sterling revered Montaigne, that the only book signed by Shakespeare is John Florio's *Montaigne* (the authority of this autograph is now doubted), and that Lord Byron regarded Montaigne as supremely im-portant. Then Emerson sketches Montaigne's life, portraying the man as frank, honest, brave, independent, and well bal-anced. The hate of his life was "color or pretence," i.e., phoni-ness. Emerson also loves Montaigne for his sincere diction. "I know not anywhere the book that seems less written. It is the language of conversation transferred to a book. Cut these words, and they would bleed; they are vascular and alive." And Emerson delightedly reports that Montaigne rarely be-came enthusiastic but did do so in expressing his love for Socrates.

Emerson quickly gets into the second half of his essay by criticizing the skeptic for the dispiriting effect his message has. "We love whatever affirms, connects, preserves; and dis-like what scatters or pulls down." Too often the noncon-formist and the rebel are equipped only "with axe and crow-bar," and not also a "plan of house or state of their own." Nonetheless the skeptic is valuable, and it behooves Emerson to address himself to the skeptic's bleakest doubts and negations. "I shall take the worst I can find [Emerson vows], whether I can dispose of them or they of me." First, the skeptic doubts that we can amass knowledge. Second, he disturbingly surrenders to fate, asking this: "What can I do against the influence of Race, in my history? What can I do against heredity and constitutional habits; against scrofula, lymph, impotence? against climate, against barbarism, in my country?" (This is a classic early consideration of the excesses of naturalism, which Emerson partially refutes in his essay "Fate.") Third, the skeptic calls life illusory and points out the chasm between theory and practice, ambition and accomplishment. "So vast is the disproportion between the sky of law and the pismire of performance under it, that whether he [any person] is a man of worth or a sot is not so great a matter as we say." Emerson concludes this section by praising the honest doubter: ". . . he denies out of more faith, and not less. He denies out of honesty. He had rather stand charged with the imbecility of skepticism, than with untruth." As such the skeptic is challenging. We should not call him a cold infidel.

But at the end Emerson returns to his position as a believer in the supremacy of moral sentiment, which enables us to "behold with serenity the yawning gulf between the ambition of man and his power of performance, between the demand and supply of power, which makes the tragedy of all souls." Stingily thwarted though our desires are, idealism still soars and "the march of civilization" goes forward, because "the world-spirit is a good swimmer, and storms and waves cannot drown him . . . Through the years and the centuries, through evil agents, through toys and atoms, a great and beneficent tendency irresistibly streams."

Fate

"Fate" and "Illusions" are the two most important and popular essays from Emerson's 1860 book called *The Conduct of Life*. "Fate" was given as a lecture in several forms beginning almost a decade before it was finally reworked and published as the first essay in the book. This long essay is an outstanding example of Emerson's dialectical method: in the first part we have a protracted statement of the position of the determinists; the short middle section contains a brief refutation, a statement for freedom through thought and conscious moral conduct; the last part, exactly balancing the first in length, subtly distinguishes between man's obviously hampering physical limitations on the one hand and his potential moral and intellectual freedom on the other. Early in the essay Emerson gives away his dialectical method by writing as follows: "This is true, and that is true . . . and then comes some reasonable hope of harmonizing them." "Fate" is one of Emerson's most splendid essays.

With tremendous energy Emerson begins by putting the case for determinism. As soon as we try to live according to a plan, "we come upon immovable limitations." So we decide at once that Fate legislates in this world. America needs to learn this quickly. "Great men, great nations, have not been boasters and buffoons, but perceivers of the terror of life, and have manned themselves to face it." Greeks, Turks, Arabs, Persians, Hindus, Calvinists, Chaucer, and savages have all believed in fatalism. "Nature is no sentimentalist . . . and will not mind drowning a man or a woman, but swallows your ship like a grain of dust." Vicious animals, droughts, earthquakes, pestilence, and the like teach us that "Providence has a wild, rough, incalculable road to its end, and it is of no use to try to whitewash its huge, mixed instrumentalities, or to dress up that terrific benefactor in a clean shirt and white neckcloth of a student in divinity."

Nature also hampers us through heredity and temperament. Even the dullest among us can read lines of certain characteristics on the human face. The theory of the four temperaments makes some sense even today. We often recognize the traits of a person's ancestors in his appearance and conduct. "Men are what their mothers made them." Further, their work helps to condition them. "You may as well ask a loom which weaves huckabuck why it does not make cashmere, as expect poetry from this engineer, or a chemical discovery from that jobber." Some people are naturally sensual. "In certain men digestion and sex absorb the vital force, and the stronger these are, the individual is so much weaker." Meanwhile, others "are born with the moral . . . bias." Then Emerson hints at the force of individual character but quickly stresses its limitations. "Once we [Emerson?] thought positive power was all. Now we learn that negative power, or circumstance, is half." In nature's book of fate, power—individual and collective—is opposed by circumstance; "when [even] a race has lived its term, it comes no more again." Opposition to fate by one person or by a whole nation seems puny and trifling: "The force with which we resist these torrents of tendency looks so ridiculously inadequate that it amounts to little more than a criticism or protest made by a minority of one, under compulsion of millions." Finally here, Emerson suggests that there is a kind of rude compensatory justice in the operation of circumstance: ". . . Fate appears as vindicator, levelling the high, lifting the low, requiring justice in man, and always striking soon or late when justice is not done." From the cosmic point of view, the individual's insight and free will are aspects of fate itself.

Now Emerson turns the coin over and briefly points out

that "Fate has its lord. . . . For though Fate is immense, so
is Power, which is the other fact of the dual world, immense."
Opposite "elemental order" are thought and spirit. To propo-
nents of fatalism, one's answer should be: ". . . a part of Fate
is the freedom of man. Forever wells up the impulse of
choosing and acting in the soul. Intellect annuls Fate. So far
as a man thinks, he is free." Further, let those who believe
in luck anticipate good luck. Emerson enumerates two specific
areas in which man is free. (1) Creative thought enables us
to oppose facts. "Just as much intellect as you add, so much
organic power." (2) The moral sentiment makes us free.
"The one serious and formidable thing in nature is a will.
. . . One way is right to go; the hero sees it, and moves on
that aim, and has the world under him for root and support."
And the hero can encourage others to be likewise heroic.

In the neatly balanced last section, Emerson spins the
coin and skillfully blends physical limitation on the obverse
with moral and intellectual freedom on the reverse. As we
mature we make fate shrink. "We stand against Fate, as
children stand up against the wall in their father's house and
notch their height from year to year." Later the boy grown
man pulls down the wall and builds a bigger one. Fate is often
simply what we do not understand; increased knowledge
diminishes fate and adds to the individual's power. Thus
"Fate is unpenetrated causes." What used to harm man
fatally, man now controls. "The mischievous torrent is taught
to drudge for man; the wild beasts he makes useful for food,
or dress, or labor; the chemic explosions are controlled like
his watch. These are now the steeds on which he rides." And
so it is with personal defects. "A transcendent talent draws so
largely on his forces as to lame him; a defect pays him reve-
nues on the other side. The sufferance which is the badge of
the Jew, has made him, in these days, the ruler of the rulers

of the earth. If Fate is ore and quarry, if evil is good in the making, if limitation is power that shall be, if calamities, oppositions, and weights are wings and means,—we are reconciled." If misfortune spurs the individual to daring choices, then obviously "fate slides into freedom and freedom into fate." The environmental balances in nature illustrate this: where there is light, eyes develop; water, fins; air, wings; and "Every zone has its own *Fauna*." The same process goes on in the social and intellectual environment. "When there is something to be done, the world knows how to do it. . . . Dante and Columbus were Italians, in their time; they would be Russians or Americans to-day [so Emerson wrote in 1860!]. Things ripen, new men come." Nor should we simply say that circumstances evoke our heroes. Instead, "Person makes event, and event person." Emerson explains in more detail: ". . . the soul contains the event that shall befall it; for the event is only the actualization of its thought, and what we pray to ourselves for is always granted." In a very modern way, Emerson goes on to suggest that people cause their lucky breaks and their accidents. "A man's fortunes are the fruit of his character. A man's friends are his magnetisms. . . . [and] the efforts which we make to escape from our destiny only serve to lead us into it." In the long run, people "meet the persons they seek"; therefore we should be careful "to ask only for high things." Emerson rambles a little here and then concludes, much in the spirit of his early essay "Nature," that we should praise "the Blessed Unity which holds nature [outer reality] and souls [inner nature] in perfect solution, and compels every atom to serve an universal end." Further, we should worship "the Beautiful Necessity," which makes all freedom contingent and limited, since without necessity "a child's hand could pull down the sun," that is, the human will would otherwise degenerate into wilfulness and license.

Illusions

"Illusions" is a short, highly poetic essay, the last one in *The Conduct of Life.* "Illusions" is about three topics, the illusory quality of fragmentary experience, the necessity that the wise man see through the mists of illusion to the mountains of truth beyond, and the resulting awareness of "the essential identity" which links all variety. The essay owes much to Emerson's reading in Hindu scriptures. Its sonorous style, which effectively blends disparate elements from "Nature" through "Experience," combined with its position in Emerson's works, gives it a benedictory quality which is most moving.

Emerson begins dramatically by describing his experience in the Mammoth Cave of Kentucky. He and his congenial party were led deep underground, the lanterns apparently were all extinguished, and by a "theatrical trick" the ceiling of the "Star-Chamber" seemed to become fretted with stars. The illusion was managed by hidden lights. Then comes the inevitable moral: "The same interference from our organization creates the most of our pleasure and pain." Our imaginations, admirations, and sentiments create "heaps of illusions" about us. We insist upon illusions. "The world rolls, the din of life is never hushed. . . . The unities, the fictions of the piece it would be an impertinence to break. . . . I find men [Emerson adds] victims of illusion in all parts of life. Children, youths, adults and old men, all are led by one bawble or another. . . . We wake from one dream into another dream."

But "now and then a sad-eyed boy"—such as Emerson— comes along and, piercing illusory appearances, is able to see the root of reality. Such critics see through human behavior to the prejudices which motivate it, whether the person thus scrutinized is a State Fair pear judge, an anti-religious humorist, a temperance-pledge signer, a Bible-society member, a dog-chaser, a chestnut gatherer, or a spouse and parent. However, Emerson quickly includes himself among those capable of irrational thought.

> I, who have all my life heard any number of orations and debates, read poems and miscellaneous books, conversed with many geniuses, am still the victim of any new page; and if Marmaduke, or Hugh, or Moosehead [all made-up names], or any other, invent a new style or mythology, I fancy that the world will be all brave and right if dressed in these colors, which I had not thought of. Then at once I will daub with this new paint; but it will not stick. 'Tis like the cement which the peddler sells at the door; he makes broken crockery hold with it, but you can never buy of him a bit of cement which will make it hold when he is gone.

Thus, most people, even the most active and realistic, "when off duty" admit good-naturedly that there are illusions. Further, there is a rank among illusions: "We begin low with coarse masks and rise to the most subtle and beautiful." Thus, we move from tobacco, narcotics, sports, to "finer games," time, and so on. "Life will show you masks that are worth all your carnivals. Yonder mountain must migrate into your mind. The fine star-dust and nebulous blur of Orion . . . must come down and be dealt with in your household thought." Finally, "What if you shall come to discern that the play and playground of all this pompous history are radiations from yourself . . . ?"

All, all is illusory, and we must admit that "There are deceptions of the senses, deceptions of the passions, and the structural, beneficent illusions of sentiment and of the intellect."

Illusory are love, "the *succession* of thought, . . . space and time . . . our pretension of *property* and even of self-hood [and] at last, even our thoughts . . ."

Thus the would-be illusion-piercing intellect has to contend with nature, time, and thought. On what basis, therefore, can we hope to "penetrate the law of our shifting moods and susceptibility?" However, once in a while the illusions fade, or rather the mists hiding reality disappear, or we avail ourselves of a better perspective. "A sudden rise in the road shows us the system of mountains, and all the summits, which have been just as near us all the year, but quite out of mind." Immutable laws, poetic justice, and virtue shine steadily through the visions we have. Gradually our groping hands find foundations beneath illusions. "There is none but a strict and faithful dealing at home and a severe barring out of all duplicity or illusion there." Moreover, although life tricks us, "we must play no games with ourselves, but deal in our privacy with the last honesty and truth." The only true basis of sublime character is probity. "This reality is the foundation of friendship, religion, poetry, and art." The worst cheat, the illusion of illusions, is foolish striving for appearances. Riches are illusory too, and "the white man, with his brow of care, always toiling" for wealth, is a fool.

Why? The answer is Emerson's conclusion. (This conclusion relates to the end of "Nature," to "The Over-Soul," and to several of the poems, including "Each and All," "The Problem," "The Sphinx," and "Brahma.") The answer lies in identity. That which seems to scatter everything in the cosmos into varieties is illusory, because a divine cohesive force really holds everything of value together into one identity: ". . . the Hindoos, in their sacred writings, express the liveliest feeling, both of the essential identity and of that illusion which they conceive variety to be. 'The notions, *"I am,"* and *"This is mine,"* which influence mankind, are but delusions of the mother of the world. Dispel, O Lord of all creatures! the conceit of knowledge which proceeds from ignorance.' And the beatitude of man they hold to lie in being freed from fascination." The intellect is appealed to by figures of speech which imply the truth, and the will is appealed to because life hides its laws behind illusions. "But the unities of Truth and of Right are not broken by the disguise." Regardless of how truth and right are colored and distorted, they are unitary. Finally Emerson gives us one of his most rapturous conclusions:

> There is no chance and no anarchy in the universe. All is system and gradation. Every god is there sitting in his sphere. The young mortal enters the hall of the firmament; there is he alone with them alone, they pouring on him benedictions and gifts, and beckoning him up to their thrones. On the instant, and incessantly, fall snowstorms of illusions. He fancies himself in a vast crowd which sways this way and that and whose movement and doings he must obey: he fancies himself poor, orphaned, insignificant. The mad crowd drives hither and thither, now furiously commanding this thing to be done, now that. What is he that he should resist their will, and think or act for himself? Every moment new changes and new showers of deceptions to baffle and distract him. And when, by and by, for an instant, the air clears and the cloud lifts a little, there are the gods still sitting around him on their thrones,—they alone with him alone.

Carlyle, who generally appreciated Emerson's later works more than the earlier ones, because of their increasing hard-headedness, was ecstatic in his praise of *The Conduct of Life* and wrote the following beautiful commendation of "Illusions": "You have grown older, more pungent, piercing;— I never read from you before such lightning-gleamings of meaning as are to be found here. The finale of all, that of 'Illusions' falling on us like snow-showers, but again of 'the gods sitting steadfast on their thrones' all the while,—what a *Fiat Lux* is there, into the deeps of a philosophy, which the vulgar has not, which hardly three men living *have*, yet dreamt of! *Well done*, I say; and so let that matter rest."

In addition to several sermons and lectures, which are now often reprinted as essays, we have now reviewed "Nature," the long essay which Emerson published as a separate book in 1836; "Self-Reliance," "Compensation," and "The Over-Soul," from *Essays, First Series*, 1841; "The Poet," "Experience," "Politics," and "New England Reformers," from the more down-to-earth *Essays, Second Series*, 1844; "Plato" and "Montaigne," from *Representative Men*, 1850; and "Fate" and "Illusions," from *The Conduct of Life*, 1860, Emerson's last major book. With more space, we might also have glanced at the following informative essays, even though they are seldom reprinted today: "History" and "Circles" (from *Essays, First Series*); "Manners" (from *Essays, Second Series*); various essay-like chapters from *English Traits*, 1856, especially "Character" and the sketches of Coleridge, Carlyle, and Wordsworth; and "Napoleon" (from *Representative Men*). But the sermons, lectures, and essays which have now been considered assuredly represent the heady essence of Emerson's prose.

V. POETRY

In February, 1835, Emerson wrote Lydia Jackson, "I am born a poet, of a low class without doubt yet a poet. That is my nature & vocation." He was right but was too modest. He wrote poetry before he was in his teens, continued to write it through his adolescence, amused his friends at Harvard by occasional verse, was chosen class poet in 1821, published some of his own verses in the *Dial* magazine in the early 1840's, and then saw into print his first volume of poetry in 1847. Twenty years later he published *May-day and Other Pieces,* which contains relatively few substantial poems but does have three or four superb ones. After senility had attacked him, his friends published a selection of his poetry and included in it a few new pieces, usually insignificant ones. After his death more poetic fragments were found and published. In his lifetime he kept up with the production of most major contemporary poets and many minor ones. He translated some poetry from foreign languages. And his prose is often highly poetic, lyrical, gnomic, and figurative.

Some critics have lavishly praised Emerson's poetry, or at least many of his poems. Others have argued that his essays are more poetic than his verse and that his verse is usually prosaic in the worst way—being unmetrical, unmusical, harsh, transitionless, and preachy. More recently, however, a tendency has manifested itself to see phases of Emerson's career as units and his literary production—prose and poetry—in those phases as unified; moreover, arguers for this position suggest that certain poems clarify certain essays of about the same date, and vice versa.

In content Emerson's poems fall into several major classes: poems for public, patriotic occasions ("Concord Hymn," "Boston Hymn," "Voluntaries," and the like); nature poems ("Berrying," "The Rhodora," "The Snow-Storm," "Woodnotes," "Musketaquid," "May-day," "The Adirondacs," "My Garden," "The Titmouse," "Seashore," and so on); personal poems ("To Ellen," "Thine Eyes Still Shined," "Threnody," "Terminus," "Grace," and parts of other poems in other categories); and poems concerning religious, aesthetic, political, and general philosophy ("The Sphinx," "Each and All," "The Problem," "Uriel," "Hamatreya," "Ode Inscribed to W. H. Channing," "Give All to Love," "Initial, Dæmonic, and Celestial Love," "Merlin," "Bacchus," "Saadi," "Brahma," "Days," "Two Rivers," and "Waldeinsamkeit"). Naturally many of the poems named, as well as dozens not named, fit into more than a single category.

A survey of more than a score of anthologies containing selected poems by Emerson shows the following to be the ten most popular, given in the order in which they were first published in book form: "Each and All," "The Problem," "Hamatreya," "The Rhodora," "The Snow-Storm," "Ode Inscribed to W. H. Channing," "Brahma," "Concord Hymn," "Days," and "Terminus." Also frequently reprinted are these next ten, again in the order of book appearance: "Uriel," "The Sphinx," "The Humble-Bee," "Woodnotes," "Give All to Love," "Merlin," "Bacchus," "Threnody," "Grace," and "Two Rivers." In addition, several other poems, although less often reprinted, are occasionally quoted or analyzed for their revealing content or style.

Many adjectives have been used to describe the style and form of Emerson's poems—for example, they have been called cryptic, didactic, ironic, searching, symbolic, and organic. Missing from such lists are words like musical, lyrical, emotional, gentle, relaxing, and the like. Most readers would agree that Emerson's poetry is highly intellectualized, often terse to the point of being epigrammatic, utterly sincere, with the form organically suited to the substance, and sometimes memorably haunting with great depths beneath seemingly simple lines. Those familiar with both Emerson's poetry and his prose know well that one mind, concerned with one array of philosophical problems, is behind the works in both genres. The poetry is simply more imaginative and symbolic; the essays, more logical and rhetorical. In his own lifetime, Emerson was so well known as a lecturer and essayist, and he was so unwilling to step forth as a national bard, that his poetry was not much appreciated. In addition, like the poetry of Poe, Whitman, and Emily Dickinson at roughly the same time, Emerson's verse was not what the public wanted. It was technically daring and did not deal with simple, emotional, human situations, as did most of William Cullen Bryant's, Henry Wadsworth Longfellow's, and John Greenleaf Whittier's. Today, however, Emerson is considered to be one of the five or six most important poets of nineteenth-century America.

Each and All

This poem, in irregular iambic tetrameter and mostly in couplets, concerns the aesthetic truism, frequently considered in Emerson's early journals, that an item of beauty is enhanced by its accompaniment or environment, indeed is not beautiful when taken from its locale. The first quarter of the poem describes a human scene full of disparate elements (separate "eaches")—field worker, heifer, and you on the hilltop—then another such scene—sexton, Napoleon, Alpine soldiers—then suggests that you may not know how inspiring your example is to your neighbor. The first section moves from sensuous perceptions to the following moral comment:

> All are needed by each one;
> Nothing is fair or good alone.

The middle section of the poem has three exempla illustrating the comment. Liking its song, the poet takes a sparrow from its nest and brings it home; but its song is cheerless, "For I did not bring home the river and sky." The same with some pretty shells taken from the shore. Their beauty depends upon nearby waves, the sounding sea, weeds, and foam; and away from such an environment, they are "poor, unsightly, noisome things." And so with a lover's "graceful maid"; taken from "the snow-white choir" of her friends, she becomes "A gentle wife, but fairy none." The final quarter of the poem follows. Momentarily disillusioned, the poet says that he prefers truth to beauty, which is only "childhood's cheat." But then he looks about him, and it appears that he is in a beautifully unified natural scene, with ground-pines, club-moss burrs, violets, oaks, firs, pine-cones, and acorns, and over all "soared the eternal sky." Comprehending the unity of truth and beauty in God's system of interdependent parts, the poet now concludes:

> Again I saw, again I heard,
> The rolling river, the morning bird;—
> Beauty through my senses stole;
> I yielded myself to the perfect whole.

The poem starts *in medias res,* and only toward the end do we realize the setting in which the poet is thinking toward his conclusion; it moves from the personal and hence limited point of view of the individual toward a more religious, philosophical position. It is notable that at the end the poet remembers bird and river, but the "graceful maid" evidently is forgotten. Nature seems ultimately more important than society here; thus the poem supports several comments in the essays "Nature," "The American Scholar," and "Self-Reliance."

The Problem

In 1832 Emerson resigned from the ministry to become a lecturer and a man of letters. Yet he always revered the sincere man of God. Why?

> Why should the vest on him allure,
> Which I could not on me endure?

This was his problem, and the poem takes its impulse from it. Emerson states his problem early and late in the poem, but he implies his solution to the problem only in the main body. He begins by stating his love of churches, churchmen, and "monastic aisles" which fall on his heart "like sweet strains, or pensive smiles." Yet he cannot be the cowled churchman whom he looks at with such respect. Why not? The implicit solution is that, given the divine origin of all beauty—man-made as well as natural—one is perhaps a man of God if he simply worships and enhances the beauty of art and of nature. God assuredly inspired Phidias when he carved his statue of Jove, the Delphic oracle when he spoke, the Bible, litanies, and canticles. Divinely inspired too was the man whose hand shaped St. Peter's dome, for

> Himself from God he could not free;
> He builded better than he knew;—
> The conscious stone to beauty grew.

Later Emerson adds the following similar thought:

> These temples grew as grows the grass;
> Art might obey, but not surpass.

It is evidently because such buildings "grew" out of the mind of God that their aesthetic form is organic—that is, alive, functional, with parts vitally interrelated. And so with elements in nature—birds' nests, shells of fish, and pine leaves, for example, build out organically from a vital center. Next, Emerson points out that man-made beauty and natural beauty are interrelated:

> Earth proudly wears the Parthenon,
> As the best gem upon her zone,
> And Morning opes with haste her lids
> To gaze upon the Pyramids;
> O'er England's abbeys bends the sky,
> As on its friends, with kindred eye.

Then Emerson reiterates and finally concludes. He implies that since the same divine spirit responsible for the beauties of nature inspires the artist's hand, one can be a man of God without wearing a cowl. Emerson greatly admires Chrysostom (John of Antioch), St. Augustine, and especially the seventeenth-century Jeremy Taylor, all superb churchmen. Yet he would not exchange places with any of them. "The Problem" is notable for its freedom from dogma (thus relating to comments in "The Lord's Supper"), for thoughts and hints concerning the romantic theory of organic art (relating to parts of "Nature," "Beauty," and "The Poet"), and for its supple iambic tetrameter verse form which includes numerous off-rhymes—for example, cowl-soul, fell-oracle, adds-myriads, etc.

Uriel

This is one of Emerson's most important Orientally inspired poems. The key to it is the realization that Emerson is being allegorically autobiographical here. The story of the poem concerns Uriel (the solar archangel in Milton's *Paradise*

Lost), a demi-god in heaven who asserted that good and
evil are relative, not absolute. The conventional deities who
heard him tried to make him suffer. But from time to time
remembrances of Uriel's message, and the occasional sound
of his voice later, make the old gods shake inexplicably. The
poem is basically iambic tetrameter but with many truncated,
trochaic lines, in occasionally irregular couplets except for the
four-line introduction. The wise but non-participating Persian
poet Saadi (about whom Emerson wrote a separate poem
called "Saadi") overhears the philosophical "lapse of Uriel,"
which occurs while

> The young deities discussed
> Laws of form, and metre just,
> Orbs, quintessence, and sunbeams,
> What subsisteth, and what seems.

Enter Uriel, "with low tones that decide." He "stirred the
devils everywhere" by his profound comments on physical and
ethical relativity.

> "Line in nature is not found;
> Unit and universe are round;
> In vain produced, all rays return;
> Evil will bless, and ice will burn."

At this pronouncement, "The stern old war-gods shook their
heads" and "The seraphs frowned," because

> The balance-beam of Fate was bent;
> The bounds of good and ill were rent;
> Strong Hades could not keep his own,
> But all slid to confusion.

Uriel must suffer for his heretical statement. His beauty
withers, and he withdraws into his cloud; "a forgetting wind"

steals over his auditors, and their lips are silent. However, since "in ashes the fire-seed [of truth] slept," occasionally "truth-speaking things" shrill out his message concerning "good of evil born," which frightens and shames the old gods. Without insisting on an exclusively autobiographical interpretation, several critics have noted that Uriel is to be equated with young Emerson, the minister who resigned and later upset the Cambridge Divinity School with his seemingly heretical address; the young deities resemble the young ministerial students who heard Emerson; and the stern if later blushing war-gods represent the conservative ecclesiasts who inevitably disapproved of Emerson's persuasive doctrine. The poem is notable for its strong, relentless meter, its superbly sustained symbolism, and its quiet humor. "Uriel" obviously relates to Emerson's "Lord's Supper," "Divinity School Address," "Compensation," "Circles," and several other essays.

The Sphinx

This poem is sphinx-like in appearance, while in reality it is eternally puzzling. Its basic iambic and anapestic dimeter gives a seemingly specious appearance of simplicity which is in keeping with the masked thought behind the poem. It has sixteen and a half eight-line stanzas. The first half of the first stanza is introductory and describes the sphinx as seemingly drowsy and brooding. She then challenges all comers to " 'tell me my secret,/The ages have kept.' " She goes on for seven full stanzas castigating man, who

> ". . . crouches and blushes,
>   Absconds and conceals;
> He creepeth and peepeth,
>   He palters and steals;
> Infirm, melancholy,

> Jealous glancing around,
> An oaf, an accomplice,
> He poisons the ground."

Nor can man make sense out of the variety and cyclical changes of nature. But the child can:

> "The babe by its mother
> Lies bathèd in joy;
> Glides its hours uncounted,—
> The sun is its toy . . ."

The sphinx then concludes by quoting man's " 'great mother,' " —that is, nature—who is concerned that her son has been confused by life and reality:

> " 'Who has drugged my boy's cup?
> Who has mixed my boy's bread?
> Who, with sadness and madness,
> Has turned my child's head?' "

The reader may become confused here, because the sphinx is at this point both the mouthpiece for nature and a kind of symbol of man's question-putting propensity. At exactly the middle of the poem, as the ninth stanza begins, we read

> I heard a poet answer
> Aloud and cheerfully,
> "Say on, sweet sphinx! thy dirges
> Are pleasant songs to me. . . ."

The last half of the poem is this poet's attempted answer to the puzzling sphinx. The answer is simply Emerson's old Oriental song about the actual identity of seemingly separate and varied elements (which he writes about in "Nature," "The Over-Soul," "Circles," "The Poet," "Plato," "Illusions," and elsewhere in prose and poetry):

"Eterne alternation
  Now follows, now flies;
And under pain, pleasure,—
  Under pleasure, pain lies.
Love works at the centre,
  Heart-heaving alway;
Forth speed the strong pulses
  To the borders of day."

The following journal entries (1859) help to clarify the
message: "The mask of Nature is variety; our education is
through surfaces and particulars; and multitudes remain in
the babe or animal state, and never see or know more: but
in the measure in which there is wit, we learn that we are
alike; that a fundamental unity or agreement exists, without
which there could be neither marriage, nor politics, nor
literature, nor science." And also this: "The perception of
identity unites all things and explains one by another, and
the most rare and strange is equally facile as the most common. But if the mind live only in particulars, and see only
differences (wanting the power to see the whole—all in each),
then the world addresses to this mind a question it cannot
answer, and each new fact tears it in pieces and it is van-
quished by the distracting variety." When the poet in "The
Sphinx" names the "Dull Sphinx," she bites her lip and
angrily asks, " 'Who taught thee me to name?' " and argues
in cacophonous diction that she and the poet are linked: " 'Of
thine eye I am eyebeam.' " She goes on to call him " 'the
unanswered question,' " adding that " 'each answer is a lie.' "
Then the sphinx merrily rises, dissolves into the clouds and the
moon, and into other ingredients of nature, saying for
conclusion that

> "Who telleth one of my meanings
> Is master of all I am."

But does the poet's answer really solve anything? The poet (if not Emerson) thinks so, feeling that in identifying the sphinx and explaining that there is a unity at the foundation of varied reality he has freed her. But some critics, looking beyond the poem to several of Emerson's other writings, especially essays like "Circles," "Plato," and "Montaigne," suggest that the sphinx leaves one challenging form only to assume another—"yellow flame," "blossoms red," even "Monadnoc's head"—equally insoluble by questing but finite man.

Hamatreya

Like many of Emerson's poems, "Hamatreya" presents contrasting points of view: first, that of the proud farmer who likes to amass much land; and second, that of the earth, which really is all that endures, while landowner after landowner dies and is buried in "his" land. The first part, which is a little less than half the poem, is in irregular, occasionally prosaic blank verse, a form which Emerson used sparingly but well (see "The Snow-Storm" and "Days"). The second part, composed of highly irregular one-, two-, and three-beat lines, quickly follows with its terse refutation of the landowners. Emerson opens the poem with a prosy list of Concord farmers (including some of his own ancestors), then a list of crops which the fruitful land has yielded. Each passing landlord was proud of his acreage and sought to add to it;

> They added ridge to valley, brook to pond,
> And sighed for all that that bounded their domain.

To increase the coming irony, Emerson quotes their complacent comments directly: " ' 'Tis mine, my children's and my name's.' " " 'This suits me for a pasture; that's my park.' " And most arrogantly:

> " 'Tis good, when you have crossed the sea and back,
>   To find the sitfast acres where you left them."

(Emerson, human being that he was, must have felt the same way upon returning from Europe on three separate occasions.) But suddenly, saying wryly that death only adds each landowner to the land, "a lump of mould the more," Emerson introduces the "Earth-Song," which begins thus:

> "Mine and yours;
>   Mine, not yours.
>   Earth endures."

Aged men are babes compared to the old sea and its old shores. Legal papers do not secure a landlord against death. Inheritors of the land are swept away, but the shaggy woodland abides. And the spirit of the earth concludes with shrewd Yankee irony:

> "They called me theirs,
>
> .   .   .   .   .   .
>
> How am I theirs,
>   If they cannot hold me,
>   But I hold them?"

Such a pronouncement cools the avarice of the narrator "Like lust in the chill of the grave." The inspiration for this characteristic Transcendental poem came from Emerson's reading of *The Vishnú Puráña*, in which Maitreya (which name Emerson unaccountably changes to "Hamatreya") is lectured on the folly of those who think that they can retain possession of things for long. Emerson copied into his journal late in

1845 pertinent passages from *The Vishnú Puráńa,* from which the following are extracts:

> "These, and other kings who with perishable frames have possessed this ever-enduring world, and who, blinded with deceptive notions of individual occupation, have indulged the feeling that suggests 'This earth is mine,—it is my son's,—it belongs to my dynasty,'—have all passed away. . . . Earth laughs, as if smiling with autumnal flowers to behold her kings unable to effect the subjugation of themselves. I will repeat to you, Maitreya, the stanzas that were chanted by Earth . . .:—
>
> " 'How great is the folly of princes . . . Foolishness has been the character of every king who has boasted, "All this earth is mine—everything is mine—it will be in my house for ever";—for he is dead. . . . When I hear a king sending word to another by his ambassador, "This earth is mine; resign your pretensions to it,"—I am at first moved to violent laughter; but it soon subsides to pity for the infatuated fool.'
>
> "These were the verses, Maitreya, which Earth recited and by listening to which ambition fades away like snow before the sun."

In its anti-materialism, "Hamatreya" relates to much in "The American Scholar," "Self-Reliance," "Compensation," and "Farming."

The Rhodora: On Being Asked, Whence Is the Flower?

This stately, dignified little poem, in heroic couplets with variations and almost as condensed as a sonnet, is one of Emerson's most traditional in form and content. In May the poet finds a beautiful rhodora in the damp, chilly woods blooming away simply "To please the desert and the sluggish brook." It is neatly pictured. The contrasting second half of the poem is devoted to the teleological moral:

> Rhodora! if the sages ask thee why
> This charm is wasted on the earth and sky,
> Tell them, dear, that if eyes were made for seeing,
> Then Beauty is its own excuse for being.

And the poet concludes by leaving the company of "sages" and happily linking himself to the uncomplicated symbol of natural beauty:

> . . . in my simple ignorance, [I] suppose
> The self-same Power that brought me there brought you.

Savoring thus the beauty of a flower stimulates the poet to an awareness of the unitary quality of all things under God's heaven. The poem is later echoed in the early part of the essay "Nature."

The Humble-Bee

This poem has six stanzas of irregular lengths (from eight to twelve lines each), with very irregular meters, and with a couplet pattern freely varied from, especially at first. It is likely that this irregularity is intentional and echoes the capricious zig-zag course of the bumble-bee itself. Emerson's purpose in calling the bee a humble-bee probably was to suggest his own intention to stay humbly near nature, like a well-adjusted bee, instead of scurrying about with purposelessness the way many people were doing in the panic year of 1837, when the poem was composed. The first stanza is notable for a magnificent pattern of assonance and dissonance which positively hums: in the first five lines, there are seven -ē sounds (bee, me, Rique, heats, seas, seek, and thee), and in

two other lines we have vowel sounds combining in a con-
trapuntal fashion ("Far-off heats through seas to seek" and
"Keep me nearer, me thy hearer"). The second stanza is
adazzle with metaphysical conceits: the bee is likened to lover,
sailor, swimmer, voyager, and epicurean. The third stanza reveals a fine contrast of movement: slow at first ("When the
south wind, in May days") in the absence of the bee, and
then faster when the bee ("Rover of the underwoods") is
heard again ("With [its] mellow, breezy bass"). The point
of the brief third stanza is simply that the bee tells only of
idleness. The fourth stanza elaborates the picture of the bee,
which here is said to see nothing "unsavory" or "unclean";
in addition, this stanza is marked by a splendid array of dis-
sonant vowels, a pattern of ă sounds, and alliteration in one
line: "Grass with green flag half-mast high." The passing bee
touches into an aesthetic picture all the wasteland which it
zig-zags through:

> All beside was unknown waste,
> All was picture as he passed.

Finally, the sixth stanza makes the irresponsible point, probably appealing to soft Transcendentalists (which Emerson
almost never was), that the bee, "Seeing only what is fair"
and "Sipping only what is sweet," is therefore "Wiser far
than human seer." The bee mocks at fate and care, and when
the cold wind blows it goes to sleep:

> Woe and want thou canst outsleep;
> Want and woe, which torture us,
> Thy sleep makes ridiculous.

The author of "Experience" knew better. In this poem he is
simply taking a philosopher's holiday. But once again, as in

"The Sphinx" (and the essays "Montaigne" and "Illusions"), Emerson may be implying an opposite meaning: is the poet like a bee, instinctively hiving beauty like honey for the delectation of those who follow and need nourishment? Such a question is probably too ingenious, but it may well have been part of Emerson's intention to raise it in his readers' minds.

The Snow-Storm

This seemingly simple blank-verse lyric, which is Emerson's earliest really fine poem, moves smoothly from a vigorous description of the dazzlingly powerful snowstorm, in the first stanza, to sustained philosophical praise, in the longer second stanza, of the artistic power of the storm—"the fierce artificer." When "the trumpets of the sky" first announce the approaching storm, whose whirlwind of snow hides everything, the farm family is content to stay inside and be snowbound (Whittier quotes part of this poem as an epigraph to his "Snow-Bound"):

> Around the radiant fireplace, enclosed
> In a tumultuous privacy of storm.

But in the second stanza the family looks out the next morning upon a new world, designed, built, and decorated by a divine architect in a single night. Note the number of words which go to make up the master metaphor of the storm as a builder: masonry, quarry, tile, bastions, myriad-handed, Parian, night-work, and architecture. No matter how gifted the human artist is, he can only "mimic in slow structures, stone by stone,/Built in an age," what God operating through nature can accomplish in moments. This fine little poem is notable for skillful assonance and sentence rhythms. It relates to such essays as "Nature," "The Poet," and "Illusions."

Woodnotes, I.

The first part of this two-part poem was composed about a year earlier than the second part and is somewhat simpler and more conventional. In Part I, which is more often reprinted than Part II, we have a charming four-stanza description in almost 150 lines of peaceful, provident nature and a character sketch of "a forest seer," who is minstrel, foreteller, harbinger, and lover of nature and things natural. Although it is counter to an Emerson family tradition, the conclusion is inevitable that the original of the character sketch is Emerson's close friend Thoreau: "It seemed that Nature could not raise/A plant in any secret place/. . . But he would come . . ./And tell its long-descended race." Emerson also reports that this nature-lover "In unploughed Maine . . . sought the lumberers' gang" and that when asked what power led him through "trackless thickets" he replied:

> "The watercourses were my guide;
> I travelled grateful by their side,
> Or through their channel dry;
>
> . . . .
>
> The falling waters led me,
> The foodful waters fed me,
>
> . . . .
>
> For Nature ever faithful is
> To such as trust her faithfulness."

Each of the four stanzas has a slightly different verse form. All are basically iambic, with occasional trochaic and other feet, usually in couplets. However, Stanza 1 combines dimeter and trimeter; Stanza 2 is mostly tetrameter; Stanza 3, pentameter; and Stanza 4, tetrameter and some trimeter, sometimes in ballad fashion reinforced by abab rhymes. Part I of "Wood-notes" is notable for simple metrical variety and clear, pleasant description.

Woodnotes, II.

This part is both longer (with almost 400 lines) and more representatively complex and philosophical than the first part. It is a long, occasionally broken song supposedly from the pine-tree. It is basically iambic tetrameter (a few times breaking into trochaic with the final syllable of the line missing). The effect is sing-song and monotonous. Almost never does Emerson rise here to any memorable lyric intensity. The pine-tree song is philosophical, not rhapsodic. The song begins with this abrupt rhetorical question:

> "Ancient or curious,
> Who knoweth aught of us?"

Only mountains, waters, moon, and stars are old enough to know the pine-tree. Then the pine exhorts its human auditor to abandon lord and town, come to all-providing nature to develop the virtues of attractive strength and courage, and taste the joys of solitude. If he does so,

> "He shall be happy whilst he woos,
> Muse-born, a daughter of the Muse.
> But if with gold she bind her hair,
> And deck her breast with diamond,
> Take off thine eyes, thy heart forbear,
> Though thou lie alone on the ground."

Listen to the wind's prophecy:

> "Aloft, abroad, the pæan swells;
> O wise man! hear'st thou half it tells?
> O wise man! hear'st thou the least part?"

The wind sings of the origin of things, of opposites and polarity, of mutability, of the differences between reality and appearance. And there is an "undersong," about causes and destiny. Then the pine-tree continues by advising man to abandon man-made things when he comes to nature, and instead to adapt his thoughts, pace, and diction to nature. Next the pine-tree sings of the unity which links all apparent varieties. Truth and beauty unite in nature:

> "Thou canst not wave thy staff in air,
> Or dip thy paddle in the lake,
> But it carves the bow of beauty there,
> And the ripples in rhymes the oar forsake.
> The wood is wiser far than thou;
> The wood and wave each other know
> Not unrelated, unaffied,
> But to each thought and thing allied,
> Is perfect Nature's every part,
> Rooted in the mighty Heart."

On the other hand, man is normally a defrauded orphan, bereft of faith, exiled and sick. But the pine-tree will explain how "thy hurt thou may'st divine." The answer is simply that

> "There lives no man of Nature's worth
> In the circle of the earth;
> And to thine eye the vast skies fall,
> Dire and satirical,
> On clucking hens, and prating fools,
> On thieves, on drudges, and on dolls."

There is hardly a "fit tenant" on the earth anywhere. But if the individual will only surrender to nature, she will "heal the hurts which sin has made." He must "Quit [his] friends as the dead in tomb," leave business, church, charity, and even "pedant lore." Do this,

> "And thou,—go burn thy wormy pages,—
> Shalt outsee seers, and outwit sages."

Gradually the lover of the woods, seeing nature's ever-changing forms, will pierce through them to the verities and will ultimately see the young spirit of God, pleased to play and happily changing his appearance, indifferent to time. Abruptly the Transcendental, slightly jerky song ends:

> "He is the axis of the star;
> He is the sparkle of the spar;
> He is the heart of every creature;
> He is the meaning of each feature;
> And his mind is the sky,
> Than all it holds more deep, more high."

The poem has been greatly praised for its thorough expression of Emerson's attitude toward nature. Part I, like the beginning of the essay "Nature," is concrete and down-to-earth; Part II, which is less popular, is as abstruse as the last three parts of "Nature" and such idealistic essays as "Compensation," "The Over-Soul," "The Poet," "Plato," and "Illusions," though not so tough-minded as parts of those later essays.

Ode Inscribed to W. H. Channing

This immensely popular poem is highly typical of Emerson, with its flashing insights, its terseness, its individualistic philosophy, and its lack of readily apparent unity. It memorably expresses one of the basic tenets of Transcendentalism:

> There are two laws discrete,
> Not reconciled,—
> Law for man, and law for thing.

Another tenet, that of individualism, informs the entire poem
and is only hinted at toward the beginning, when Emerson
says that if he leaves his study to deal with "the priest's cant"
and the "statesman's rant," his Muse will grow angry and
confuse him. Nonetheless, Emerson does address himself to
cant and rant. The poem falls into four seemingly unrelated
parts. The first two brief stanzas explain that Emerson is
reluctant to cause any grief to William Henry Channing
(1810-1884), Transcendentalist, abolitionist, and reformer, who
was especially vocal during the Mexican War. But if Emerson
strays from his chosen work, he will grow confused. The next
four stanzas are a snarling condemnation of "the famous
States" which are now harrying Mexico. An undersong im-
plicitly condemns such statesmen as Daniel Webster. The
North need not boast, since it is filled with "jackals" pursuing runaway slaves. Emerson then compares "the lofty
land" to an oak and the people to bats and wrens housing
themselves there. Next he taunts the Northerners who have
threatened to secede; the same old end, that of materialism,
would still be served. In the next four stanzas Emerson casti-
gates this pervasive spirit of materialism, most violently in this
stanza:

> The horseman serves the horse,
> The neatherd serves the neat,
> The merchant serves his purse,
> The eater serves his meat;
> 'Tis the day of the chattel,
> Web to weave, and corn to grind;
> Things are in the saddle,
> And ride mankind.

He goes on to say that while those who follow "law for
thing" build towns and fleets, man is unkinged in the process.

" 'Tis fit the forest fall," the land be tilled, steamers be built, and so on; but "Let man serve law for man" and live for friendship, love, truth, and harmony, and the state will take care of itself. Not wishing to end his poem negatively or cynically, Emerson adds two stanzas full of positive advice and then hope.

> Every one to his chosen work;—
> Foolish hands may mix and mar . . .

And finally,

> The over-god
> Who marries Right to Might,

will bring honey out of the lion and even see to it that when a land is unjustly overrun and conquered, the victors will divide into two bands.

> Half for freedom strike and stand;—
> The astonished Muse finds thousands at her side.

Thus Emerson characteristically answers reformers who urged him to help them. Each must work in his own way, pointing out in his own works the wrongs that he sees but always hoping for the best. In content the poem relates to "The American Scholar," "Self-Reliance," "Compensation," "Politics," and "New England Reformers." In its frank and unresolved statement of one man's dilemma—how can one remain idealistic when the times are out of joint?—it is typical of most of Emerson's literary works.

Give All to Love

This is a poem about love but is not a love poem. Through its having first a statement about the pleasure of knowing that one is loved, and then an espousal of self-reliance beyond any love of another, it is typical of Emerson's settled habit of dialectically turning over the medal to see the other side. The first half of the poem is almost a lyric praise of love. "Give all to love," because "It is a brave master" and should be followed devotedly, even beyond hope. Emerson flatters lovers:

> It [love] was never for the mean;
> It requireth courage stout.

But as the fourth of the six stanzas of the poem opens, we have the first tentative note of doubt, with the word "yet":

> Leave all for love;
> Yet, hear me, yet . . .

And then the sobering advice: "Keep thee . . ./Free . . ./ Of thy beloved." The second line of the fifth stanza emphasizes the more mature philosophy, beginning with the word "but":

> Cling with life to the maid;
> But . . .

when she is aware, as she must grow independent enough to be, "Of a joy apart from thee," then she is free. The last stanza presents this thoroughly Emersonian self-reliant and compensation-seeking attitude:

> Heartily know,
> When half-gods go,
> The gods arrive.

The author of the essays "Self-Reliance," "Compensation," "Love," "Experience," "Fate," and "Illusions," as well as the poem "Initial, Dæmonic, and Celestial Love," could do no less than advise us to believe that those whom Venus joins, inevitable individualism must separate.

Merlin

Emerson does not have King Arthur's Merlin in mind here, nor even the legendary Welsh bard Merlin, so much as a kind of ideal heroic bard. (Similarly in "Saadi" he writes less of the Persian poet Saadi than of his archetype of the poet.) Emerson's bard is ideally a wild, grand singer whose message urges its listeners along the path of goodness and nobility. The poem is complex and subtle. In Part I, which is a little longer than Part II, Emerson through Merlin defines serious poetry.

> Thy trivial harp will never please
> Or fill my craving ear;
> Its chords should ring as blows the breeze,
> Free, peremptory, clear.

Emerson may well have Poe in mind in the following critical lines:

> No jingling serenader's art,
> Nor tinkle of piano strings,
> Can make the wild blood start
> In its mystic springs.

Instead, the "kingly bard" must be tough and hammer out his music, making it chime "with the forest tone," flood, oratory, city din, war and brave marching, and martyrs' prayers. (Here Emerson seems to be calling for a Whitman, as he does in his essay "The Poet.") So much for tone and content. Now for bardic form:

> He shall not his brain encumber
> With the coil of rhyme and number;

But leaving rule and pale forethought,
He shall aye climb
For his rhyme.

(Emerson could never free himself of "the coil" of rhythm and rhyme to the extent that Whitman and, later, Emily Dickinson did.) Again (as in the essay "The Poet") Emerson espouses the theory that the argument of the poem must determine its form:

Forms more cheerly live and go,
What time the subtle mind
Sings aloud the tune whereto
Their pulses beat,
And march their feet,
And their numbers are combined.

As for the true bard's purpose and effect, Emerson says that like the philosopher's writings,

Merlin's mighty line
Extremes of nature reconciled,

and makes the tyrant sensible, the lion mild, the tempest still, the land fertile, and—most important—"bring[s] in poetic peace." The true poet does not temporize, will not weave efficacious rhymes in weak and unhappy times, but waits patiently and publishes when "the propitious mind" (perhaps God's) is so inclined. Under such circumstances, "When God's will sallies free," even a dullard could see "The flowing fortunes of a thousand years." Thus the ideal bardic poet is in tune with nature (forest, flood, etc.), other men (orators, soldiers, etc.), and time itself. In Part II Emerson suggests that the bard is the opposite number of the king. (In "The Poet" he made a trinity of knower-doer-sayer; presumably here the poet is knower-sayer, and the king is doer.) This permits an expansion into the following general law:

> Balance-loving Nature
> Made all things in pairs.

Then Emerson proceeds to explicate this basic concept by citing the antipodes, complementary colors, harmonic notes, blending flavors, pairs of leaves and cotyledons, hands, feet, and finally "In one body grooms and brides." Even more, "every mortal" has in himself or herself "two married sides" (in his lecture "Education" Emerson contrasts "will, the male power," and "Sympathy, the female force"); and "Thoughts come also hand in hand," either "mated" or "alternated." (This suggests the unifying force of mind, discussed in "Nature," and also Emerson's later attraction toward dilemmas and paradoxes as expressed, for example, in "Experience," "Montaigne," "Fate," and "Illusions.") Suddenly leaping to a cosmic level, Emerson balances Justice and Nemesis, the former being "the rhyme of things" and the latter being the force which "with even matches odd." Behind human efforts to get beneath the sensual surface of things, fathom reality, and express it poetically (which even Merlin can do only imperfectly), the fatal cosmic singers are better bards:

> Subtle rhymes, with ruin rife,
> Murmur in the house of life,
> Sung by the Sisters as they spin;
> In perfect time and measure they
> Build and unbuild our echoing clay.
> As the two twilights of the day
> Fold us music-drunken in.

Dawn and dusk—youthful *joie de vivre* and imperfect old-age disillusion—bracket our lives, through which celestial bardic music thrills. "Merlin" is a cryptic poem and demands close reading and re-reading.

Bacchus

Bacchus may have been the god of wine, but Emerson writes here of poetic wine—that which intoxicates and releases the poet-philosopher. The poem is metrically rough, almost unscannable, with iambs giving way to many trochees and a few anapests. The rhyme-scheme quickly collapses, and after the second stanza end-sounds may or may not pick up partners later. The effect, that of a reeling dionysiac revel, is undoubtedly intentional. Emerson was partly inspired here by some of the lush poetry of the Persian poet Hafiz. The poem moves from a consideration of the nature of inspiring wine to a celebration of the power of true wine to elevate the poet. The poem becomes more and more intense as the wine of inspiration works; correspondingly, the inspired poet is increasingly released, made more expansive through space and time, and more able philosophically and philanthropically. "Bacchus" begins with a rush:

> Bring me wine, but wine which never grew
> In the belly of the grape.

The imperious speaker wants

> Wine of wine,
> Blood of the world,
> Form of forms, and mould of statures,
> That I intoxicated,
> And by the draught assimilated,
> May float at pleasure through all natures.

He mixes his sensations, wanting

Wine that is shed
Like the torrents of the sun
Up the horizon walls.

If he can only have "Wine which Music is," he can "hear far
Chaos talk" and can walk with unborn kings. Obviously what
he wants is artistic and philosophical inspiration, so that he
can pierce through appearance and achieve a vision of true
beauty for the betterment of man. Emerson concludes platonically by expressing a desire to recover an awareness once
enjoyed but now lost:

> Pour, Bacchus! the remembering wine;
> Retrieve the loss of me and mine!

The poem echoes thoughts in the essays "Nature," "The
Poet," and "Circles."

Threnody

This poem is longer than any other one by Emerson,
except for "Woodnotes." It was occasioned by the death of his
first son, Waldo, in January, 1842. Like many of Emerson's
works, in prose as well as poetry, it is a medal of upper and
under surfaces. In this case, the beginning expresses some of
Emerson's bleakest bitterness, such as we find only in his letters and the privacy of his journals. The second part is more
philosophical, and begins thus:

> The deep Heart answered, "Weepest thou?
> Worthier cause for passion wild
> If I had not taken the child. . . ."

It expresses the poet's recovery from personal misery through
a realization that his little son is now a part of all. Nature
comforts the father with these words:

"My servant Death, with solving rite,
Pours finite into infinite.
Wilt thou freeze love's tidal flow,
Whose streams through Nature circling go?"

But first comes the overflowing bitterness. The first part of "Threnody" makes three points: the boy is taken away from nature, which may be powerful but is not strong enough to quicken the dead; nature and the boy's friends can be delighted by the boy no more; and his grieving father feels partly destroyed himself. The poem opens in misery:

The South-wind brings
Life, sunshine and desire,
And on every mount and meadow
Breathes aromatic fire;
But over the dead he has no power;
The lost, the lost, he cannot restore;
And, looking over the hills, I mourn
The darling who shall not return.

The two- and three-beat lines gradually lengthen to tetrameter, occasionally shortened again later, as though the numbed poet could not always complete his lines. The "deep-eyed boy" with his eloquent voice delighted all those about him, including adults:

. . . fairest dames and bearded men,
Who heard the sweet request,
So gentle, wise and grave,
Bended with joy to his behest
And let the world's affairs go by.

Reminders of the dead lad are all about—sled, sticks, sand-pile, and "every inch of garden ground." The poet feels especially bereft when he sees that nature remains unaccountably gay:

The morrow dawned with needless glow;
Each snowbird chirped, each fowl must crow;
Each tramper started . . .

Why could "No angel from the countless host" stoop to pro-
tect that unique child? The poet never called him his, "But
Nature's heir." Perhaps the child was too perfect for ailing
nature to sustain. At all events, the father says to the spirit of
the son:

> The eager fate which carried thee
> Took the largest part of me,

and left "the world dishonored." Part II more briefly describes
the recovery of the poet, as "the deep Heart" lyrically lectures
him. Why should he think that beauty is lost? Love remains,
and the ladder of love up to heaven.

> " 'Tis not within the force of fate
> The fate-conjoined to separate. . . ."

Grief is blasphemous. After the boy's beauty filled nature for
a while, death poured "finite into infinite"; this only demonstrates the inevitable mutability of all things material and
mortal.

> "Light is light which radiates,
> Blood is blood which circulates,
> Life is life which generates,
> And many-seeming life is one,—
> Wilt thou transfix and make it none?
> Its onward force too starkly pent
> In figure, bone, and lineament?
> Wilt thou, uncalled, interrogate,
> Talker! the unreplying Fate?"

Mankind must learn that God built heaven not of "adamant and gold" but rather of reeds, grass, scented weeds, tears, sacred flames, virtue, "furtherance and pursuing,/Not of spent deeds, but of doing." When "house and tenant" sink into the ground and are lost in God, they are found in Godhead. "Threnody" is long but simple, and is notable for its dramatic movement from bitter grief to characteristically philosophical recovery.

Grace

This uncharacteristic little poem of eight slightly irregular iambic pentameter lines (rhyming ababbacc) runs counter to later essays like "Self-Reliance," "Experience," and "Fate." In it Emerson thanks the Calvinist God of his ancestors for setting around him such barriers as "Example, custom, fear, occasion slow," and says that "These scorned bondmen were my parapet." He adds that he does not dare to glance over these "defences" at "the roaring gulf below," which contains depths of sin which he would have fallen into "Had not these me against myself defended." The form and syntax of the poem are traditional, harking back to some of Emerson's favorite seventeenth-century religious poets. Although it may be ingeniously argued that God's grace is the source of all individualism, it is surely more sensible to admit that here Emerson is theologically conservative even while he is being poetically adept.

Concord Hymn

This is Emerson's most famous exoteric verse and was occasioned by a celebration on July 4, 1837, at the site of a battle monument. On a piece of land given by Emerson's step-grandfather Ezra Ripley, a monument was erected to commemorate the bravery of the minutemen who fought the

British at Concord in 1775. The poem is a fine demonstration that verse for a specific public occasion may well become immortal. It has four stanzas, each of four lines; each line has four beats. The rhyme scheme is a simple abab. The most memorable line is the one which describes "the embattled farmers" who "fired the shot heard round the world." But the entire poem is perfect of its kind. Not a syllable could be improved. It begins by telling of the farmer-soldiers "By the rude bridge." The silence of death has claimed past "foe" and "conqueror" alike,

> And Time the ruined bridge has swept
> Down the dark stream which seaward creeps.

The present act is to "set to-day a votive stone," so that

> . . . memory may their deed redeem,
> When, like our sires, our sons are gone.

Emerson skillfully moves from past to present, and he looks far into the future when he exhorts the heroic spirit which inspired the minutemen to

> Bid Time and Nature gently spare
> The shaft we raise to them and thee.

All of Emerson's poems which have been discussed up to this point were first published in book form in *Poems*, 1847. The works to be considered in detail next are from *May-day and Other Pieces*, 1867, and generally represent a slight falling off of technical versatility but with it possibly a greater degree of clear depth.

Brahma

This profound little poem in four iambic tetrameter quatrains (rhyming abab) owes its inception to Emerson's reading in Oriental scriptures and his pondering on compensation and the Over-Soul. In the autumn of 1845 Emerson copied into his journal the following quotation from H. H. Wilson's translation of the *Vishnú Purána*: "What living creature slays, or is slain? What living creature preserves or is preserved? Each is his own destroyer or preserver, as he follows evil or good." Emerson mulled this concept over for more than a decade, and then in the summer of 1856 he copied the following passages from the *Upanishads*: ". . . from him [God] none is separated; this is that. What is here, the same is there, and what is there, the same is here. He proceeds from death to death who beholds here difference. He (Brahma, or the Soul) does not move; is swifter than the mind: not the gods (the senses) did obtain him, he was gone before. Standing, he outstrips all the other gods, how fast soever they run. He is far, and also near." Emerson used many other sources, literary and personal, for his poem. There is something apt in the fact that "Brahma," Emerson's supremely fine celebration of the concept of absolute unity, is an amalgamation of countless separate elements of reading and personal thought. In showing the harmonious unity of all constituents and aspects of life, "Brahma" is similar to the poem "Each and All" (as well as such essays as "Compensation," "The Over-Soul," "Plato," and "Immortality"); but "Brahma" is unusual in being chanted by God rather than by the harmony-seeking human mind. It begins:

> If the red slayer think he slays,
>   Or if the slain think he is slain,
> They know not well the subtle ways
>   I keep, and pass, and turn again.

The Over-Soul, or pure being, or God as a creative spirit driving through all parts of the cosmos, is speaking. From such a point of view—that of a subtle, staying, moving, return-ing being—nothing can die, since all energy is conserved and merely takes different temporary embodiments. The second stanza continues the idea of the essential identity of seeming opposites, both physical and moral:

> Far or forgot to me is near;
>   Shadow and sunlight are the same;
> The vanished gods to me appear;
>   And one to me are shame and fame.

Since this creative energy is everywhere and is hence a unit, a person would be a fool to think of escaping it or even doubt-ing its existence:

> They reckon ill who leave me out;
>   When me they fly, I am the wings;
> I am the doubter and the doubt,
>   And I the hymn the Brahmin sings.

In the final stanza, Emerson writes of the "strong gods." These are Indra, the god of the sky; Agni, the god of fire; and Yama, the god of death, judgment, and immortality. These three gods ultimately become absorbed into the one god Brahma. And Emerson writes of the "sacred Seven," identified as the seven Maharshis or highest saints in the Hindu hier-archy. Partial gods and saintly human beings cannot find the home of Brahma. But a calm awareness of the coming resolu-tion of one's form into the divine being is beatific beyond any conventional dream of heaven. Emerson puts all of this with rare compression:

> The strong gods pine for my abode,
>   And pine in vain the secret Seven;
> But thou, meek lover of the good!
>   Find me, and turn thy back on heaven.

"Brahma" is notoriously difficult for most readers. Emerson sensed this and advised readers that if they would "say Jehovah instead of Brahma, they will not feel any perplexity." But such advice does not help much unless the reader has already accepted the Oriental and Platonic philosophical principle of the essential unity, and even identity, of everything in the universe.

Days

This matchless blank-verse lyric is in two parts. The first six lines personify days as semi-divine daughters of Time who offer various gifts to every man and woman. Then the last five lines become personal and sadly negative as the poet, rather Calvinistic here, confesses that he has wasted his precious time. The initial personification is skillfully sustained throughout: the "Daughters of Time" are "hypocritic" (meaning simply deceptive), "Muffled and dumb like barefoot dervishes"; they march singly in an endless line (days are not numbered, though those of an individual life are), and "To each they offer gifts after his will," from fagots to diadems, and from bread to "stars, and sky that holds them all." Emerson is poetically implying his romantic belief that the self-reliant can have anything he wants from time. In the last half of the poem, Emerson becomes personal and oddly self-critical:

I, in my pleachèd [intertwined] garden, watched the pomp,
Forgot my morning wishes, hastily
Took a few herbs and apples . . .

Then he adds that the gift-bearing day turned and left him without a word. Finally,

. . . I, too late,
Under her solemn fillet [hair-band] saw the scorn.

In "Days" Emerson presents a simple picture, with movement and color, depth and variety. He expands the pictorial image into a briefly sustained metaphor, which carries the implicit message of a parable but with none of its prosy dryness. In addition, Emerson explicitly condemns himself for time-wasting, that sin of sins to his Puritan forebears. If readers are inclined to cast rocks at Emerson for wasting time, let them do two things first: let them consider what Emerson did do with his time, and also examine their own use of their days. At the same time, we should perhaps realize that when Emerson was sitting idly in his garden apparently wasting his time, he was in reality nurturing and developing his thoughts with rare efficiency and consideration. Further, Emerson may just possibly be implying as much in his poem. In any event, "Days" challenges us to reassess what we call busy-ness and idleness.

Two Rivers

In April, 1856, Emerson was inspired by the Concord River, whose Indian name was Musketaquit (or Musketaquid), to write in his journal what almost amounted to the poem "Two Rivers" in prose. The impulse was his hearing the sweet voice of the river, which echoed the sound of the rain. But immediately he leaped to a consideration of the platonic ideal river of which the Concord is but a limited shadow. In prose Emerson wrote, "Thou art shut in thy banks; but the stream I love, flows in thy water, and flows through rocks and through the air, and through darkness, and through men, and women. . . ." Thus the physical river became for Emerson a symbol of flowing passions and thoughts. (This thinking is in keeping with the section called "Language" in the essay "Nature.") The purpose of the title "Two Rivers" is to suggest that the natural river symbolizes the spiritual one. Emerson begins the poem with a brief description of the real river's voice:

> Thy summer voice, Musketaquit,
> Repeats the music of the rain . . .

But by the third line he indicates his preference for the non-physical river which the Concord stands for:

> But sweeter rivers pulsing flit
> Through thee, as thou through Concord Plain.

The same contrast is maintained in the second stanza:

> Thou in thy narrow banks art pent:
> The stream I love unbounded goes
> Through flood and sea and firmament;
> Through light, through life, it forward flows.

The third stanza is devoted exclusively to the spiritual stream. Then the fourth, after adverting to a journal description of the jewel-like rocks at the bottom of the real river, closes with a statement that its audible song makes hearers "lose their grief." But the fifth and last stanza makes it clear that Transcendental rivers are the poet's main concern:

> So forth and brighter fares my stream,—
> Who drink it shall not thirst again;
> No darkness stains its equal gleam,
> And ages drop in it like rain.

Terminus

Terminus was the Roman god of boundaries, borders, and limits. He presumably would have been the deity to fix the terminal date of Emerson's productive life. With characteristically accurate self-knowledge, the poet, by 1866, when he read the finished poem to his startled son in New York, realized that his important working days were over. "Terminus" is in two parts. The first announces that the god of boundaries, "Who sets to seas a shore," has fatally come to the aging poet with this command:

> Contract thy firmament
> To compass of a tent.
> There's not enough for this and that,
> Make thy option which of two;
> Economize the failing river . . .

Terminus tempts Emerson to be annoyed, if he wishes, to complain that his ancestors failed to bequeath him tough sinews, but only "ebbing veins" and "nerveless reins [kidneys]" and the like. However, the poet predictably accepts his fatal decline—which, sure enough, followed in a very few years—with imperturbable serenity and an unshakable faith in compensation:

> As the bird trims her to the gale,
> I trim myself to the storm of time,
> I man the rudder, reef the sail,
> Obey the voice at eve obeyed at prime.

Beautifully, that voice of the evening exhorts him to sail ahead fearlessly, since

> "The port, well worth the cruise, is near,
> And every wave is charmed."

We have now examined Emerson's twenty most popular poems and have seen that, throughout his career as a poet, he combined metrical daring—dissonance, deliberately roughened rhythms, lines of irregular lengths, profuse imagery, and challenging symbolism—with conventional prosodial effects.

His poetic themes include every major theme developed in his lectures and essays: patriotic, political, aesthetic, and philosophical. His regular habit of thought is dialectical—to consider an idea from contrasting points of view. In the process, he reveals both his mystical and his Yankee sides. The sources of his poetic impulses are usually deep within himself, since he is stirred by nature, by his reading, by significant contemporary events, and—most often—simply by self-scrutiny.

More space would have permitted detailed consideration of the ten next most popular poems by Emerson: "Good-bye," "Mithridates," "Fable," "Forbearance," "Forerunners," "Ode to Beauty," "The Apology," "Merops," "Waldeinsamkeit," and "Thought." Other poems rarely reprinted but significant for one reason or another include "Thine Eyes Still Shined," "Initial, Dæmonic, and Celestial Love," "Saadi," "Boston Hymn," "Voluntaries," "The Romany Girl," "Seashore," "The Bohemian Hymn," several "Quatrains," and some of the epigraphs preceding the essays. However, a more thorough study of all of these other poems would probably not significantly alter one's understanding of and respect for Emerson the poet which one can achieve by a careful reading of the twenty major poems.

VI. TRANSCENDENTALISM

Even a simple approach to the complex literary and philosophical movement of Transcendentalism should take into consideration four main aspects: what the movement grew out of, who its leading thinkers were, what in general their principal beliefs were, and what practical and long-range good these people did.

Sources

The immediate cause of Transcendentalism was discontent. About 1820 various thinkers in New England and, to some extent, elsewhere in the United States began to be irritated by the dryness, materialistic smugness, and excessive rationality of Unitarianism. The Unitarians, themselves in reaction against Calvinism, believed in the brotherhood of all mankind, the inevitability of progress forever, and the possibility of individual salvation through personal character and goodness. Further, they held to the fatherhood of God and to the example of Jesus Christ, whom they regarded as a great man but not divine. All of this sounds much like Emerson, who, however, early in his life mordantly criticized what he called "corpse-cold" Unitarianism for the increasing wealth, intellectual apathy, and general conservatism of its most influential practitioners, the increasing stress by its ministers upon petty Biblical exegesis, its denial of the importance of individual soul-searching, and its emphasis upon form, ritual, and dogma. Yet as Emerson and his like-minded cohorts were breaking away from Unitarianism, a wilder and more philanthropic group of Unitarians, under the leadership of the eloquent William Ellery Channing (1780-1842), began to dominate their faith. Some of the sermons and essays of Channing in the 1820's helped to pave the way for Transcendentalism in the 1830's. Emerson began his professional career as a Unitarian minister; even after he had abandoned the pulpit to become an independent and then a Transcendentalist, he remained in his own way sympathetic with some of the beliefs of the Unitarians. Curiously, he can also be seen to have a few vestigial remains of the Calvinism of his seventeenth-century forebears, against which religion the Unitarians thoroughly rebelled.

The philosophical and literary sources of Transcendentalism are fourfold: Platonism, German idealistic philosophy, Oriental mysticism, and native American elements.

Emerson got his Platonism from Plato directly and also by way of the writings of such neo-Platonists as Plotinus and also seventeenth-century Cambridge Platonists like Ralph Cudworth. During his college years Emerson began to admire Socrates and later made him a kind of touchstone of greatness, often asking people what they thought of him and judging them by their responses. Emerson was surprised and disappointed, for example, when neither Landor nor Carlyle shared his reverence for Socrates. In his journals Emerson exhorted himself to read "Plotinus, Proclus, Porphyry, Iamblichus," among other Platonists. He regarded Plato as the archetype of the genuine philosopher; however, in his essay on Plato, the Greek takes on mystic and Oriental coloration emanating from Emerson fully as much as from anything Plato ever wrote. It might be said fairly that Emerson saw in Plato an attempt at the reconciliation of matter and spirit which Emerson himself wanted to enunciate at least as early as 1836, the date of his essay "Nature." Platonism also supported Emerson's speculations on the Over-Soul, on the soul as a microcosm of the universal soul, on the correspondences between inner and outer nature and between law for thing and law for man, and on the high function of the poet and his poetry. The influence of Platonism on Emerson, like all influences upon him, was intermittent and incomplete. It was always his habit of mind to take from a source only what corresponded to a previous thought, feeling, or need already within himself.

Just as Platonism came to Emerson partly through followers of Plato, so with German idealism, which arrived at Concord partly by way of Coleridge and Carlyle. Emerson knew no German when he first met Carlyle in Scotland. He had been urged by his brother William Emerson to study German in order to follow the latest European commentaries on Christianity, and Carlyle also strongly advised him to study the language of Schiller, Fichte, and especially Goethe. Both Coleridge and Carlyle had done much to extend the influence of German romantic literature and thought into England, and Emerson revered both Coleridge and Carlyle, and also was attuned to much of the idealism in their writings which derived partly from German sources. Margaret Fuller taught Emerson a little German, and he painfully taught himself a good bit more. But he always preferred the early Goethe to the later; and, decent New Englander that he was, he could never really excuse Goethe for his conceit and his "bad morals." Nonetheless, he recognized him for a titan: modern rebel, friend of science, literary genius, and splendid writer. Although he could never fully approve of Goethe, Emerson was the better for reading him, was made less narrow, less puritanical. In a poem called "To J.W." (John Weiss, a minister who criticized the dead Goethe), Emerson wrote as follows:

> Set not thy foot on graves;
> Nor seek to unwind the shroud
> Which charitable Time
> And Nature have allowed
> To wrap the errors of a sage sublime.

This aptly shows Emerson's opinion of Goethe, a sublime sage whose "errors" were real but should be forgotten in the light of his ultimate achievements. Emerson paid a full measure of respect to Goethe in *Representative Men* when he included a chapter in it called "Goethe; or, the Writer."

Probably the most important single source of religious and literary inspiration for Emerson was Oriental writings. Before he was out of his teens, he had begun to read Oriental literature in translation, and therefore such basic Eastern tenets as the impersonality of the deity, the relativity of evil, and the unimportance of material possessions owe their origin to his early acceptance of Oriental doctrines. His "Divinity School Address," his essays "Compensation" and "The Over-Soul," and such poems as "Uriel," "Hamatreya," and "Brahma" directly or indirectly stem from the Orientalist in him. Emerson communicated his excitement about Oriental writings to friends and followers like Thoreau, who went on to read them in their own way, write under their influence, and thus in turn re-infect Emerson. Furthermore, the Persian poets Hafiz and Saadi contributed not only some basic concepts to his thought but also a good deal of unpuritanical lushness and color to his style. Emerson regarded as his ideal poet Saadi —see the poem by that title—and much of the inspiring wine behind his poem "Bacchus" was manufactured in Persia. Emerson's lifelong favorite reading included the *Bhagavat*

Gita, Confucius, Firdousi, the *Gulistan,* Hafiz, Saadi, the *Vishnú Puráña,* and Zoroastrian literature; and when Emerson nicknamed his wife Lidian "Mine Asia" it was presumably in compliment to her harmonious completeness, strangeness, and poetic attraction.

American Transcendentalism also owed much of its moral earnestness to the Puritanism lurking in the past of many of its practitioners. In addition, Quaker intuition is much like Transcendental intuition: both Quakers and Transcendentalists saw nature as a tangible symbol corresponding to the intangible divine and to the qualities deep within every individual, who therefore could trust himself to perceive the highest truths without any mediation by churchmen or logicians.

Hence Transcendentalism is a unique compound of Platonism and neo-Platonism, German idealism, Oriental mysticism, and native American elements such as Puritanism and certain Quaker beliefs.

Leaders

Taken up in alphabetical order, the associates and near-peers of Emerson in the Transcendental movement include Bronson Alcott, Orestes Brownson, William Ellery Channing the younger, William Henry Channing, James Freeman Clarke, Christopher Pearse Cranch, Convers Francis, Margaret Fuller, Nathaniel Hawthorne, Frederic Henry Hedge, Julia Ward Howe, Theodore Parker, Elizabeth Peabody, George Ripley, Henry David Thoreau, and Jones Very. These people naturally were unequally enthusiastic and therefore contributed in different ways, sometimes very minor, to the

Transcendental movement. Emerson knew every one of them personally, and almost all of them greatly respected him.

The father of Louisa May (whose *Little Women* later helped support him), Bronson Alcott was a self-educated school-teacher with exceedingly advanced notions on education. Emerson's essay "Education" contains ideas which Alcott had long put into practice. Alcott admired Emerson's "Over-Soul" but felt that his compensatory essay "Self-Reliance" did not sufficiently stress the concept of the intellectual and spiritual oneness of all mankind. Alcott tried his own variety of communal farm living, in a vegetarian outfit called Fruitlands, which failed quickly. Emerson admired Alcott greatly, and so did Thoreau, who in *Walden* (Chapter 14) movingly described him as follows: "He is perhaps the sanest man and has the fewest crotchets of any I chance to know. . . . A blue-robed man, whose fittest roof is the overarching sky which reflects his serenity. I do not see how he can ever die; Nature cannot spare him."

Orestes Brownson was a liberal minister who vacillatingly tried Presbyterianism, Unitarianism, and Transcendentalism before finally becoming a Roman Catholic. He eloquently supported workers' rights and lived for a time at Brook Farm. He is also important for having popularized Coleridge, Carlyle, and German idealistic writers.

William Ellery Channing the younger was the nephew of the celebrated Unitarian minister W. E. Channing. Young Ellery Channing, the earthy, irresponsible son of a prominent physician, ran away from Harvard to live alone in the prairies of Illinois; this gesture and hiking trips taken with Channing inspired his friend and companion Thoreau, whose biography Channing published in 1873. Channing married Margaret Fuller's sister Ellen and later wrote several volumes of awkward but sincere nature poetry, which Emerson helped to champion.

William Henry Channing, another nephew of the redoubtable Doctor Channing, was also a radical Transcendentalist. This Channing was a Unitarian minister in Cincinnati for a few years, editing while there the *Western Messenger,* to which Emerson and many other Transcendentalists contributed. Later Channing returned to Boston to associate with the Brook Farm founders and other Fourierists. With Emerson and James Freeman Clarke, he collaborated on the *Memoirs of Margaret Fuller Ossoli.* He later lived for decades in England.

James Freeman Clarke, a product of the Harvard Divinity School, was a militant Unitarian minister in Kentucky for a few years, helping to edit the *Western Messenger.* Clarke then returned to Boston and became a prominent minister for almost half a century. He wrote several books on the essentials of religion and the need for common sense in religion. He worked with Emerson and W. H. Channing on Margaret Fuller's memoirs.

A Virginian by birth, Christopher Pearse Cranch graduated from the Harvard Divinity School and then went west after J. F. Clarke, succeeding him as a Unitarian minister in Louisville, Kentucky, and as an editor of the *Western Messenger.* Then he returned to Boston to socialize, went on to Rome and Florence and Paris for a period of thirteen years, and retired from active ministerial duty to become a pathetically idle figure. He partly wasted his immense talents as minister, painter, caricaturist, poet, translator, and literary critic.

Convers Francis was a dignified but timorous Unitarian minister who taught at the Harvard Divinity School for more than twenty years. Early in his career he helped to popularize German idealism, but when he had to choose between Transcendental principles and social ostracism on the one hand, and comfortable conformity on the other, he fell away from the movement supported by Emerson and other anti-materialists.

Margaret Fuller was a precocious, high-minded, eccentric friend of geniuses. From her earliest years she was terribly well read, especially in revolutionary writers and German idealistic men of letters. At one time she planned to write a life of her contemporary idol, Goethe. She conducted conversational classes in the home of Elizabeth Peabody, and out of this thinking emerged a book of great importance in its field, *Woman in the Nineteenth Century,* part of which first saw print in the *Dial* magazine after Emerson had succeeded Miss Fuller as its editor. She then became a literary critic for the *Tribune* under its editor Horace Greeley in New York, during which time she had the courage to attack the poetry of such Boston Brahmins as Lowell and Longfellow. She went to Europe in 1846, married a virile but unintelligent and impoverished Italian named Marquis Angelo Ossoli. They had a son. Greatly admiring the Italian patriot Giuseppe Mazzini, she became embroiled in the Roman revolution of 1848-1849 and prepared a history of it. Returning to the United States in 1850 at the age of forty, she was drowned with her husband and child off Fire Island, near New York. The manuscript of her history of the Roman revolution was lost. Margaret Fuller knew and was respected by most of the Transcendentalists. She was the most complex woman writer in America before Emily Dickinson. Emerson helped to put together Margaret Fuller's memoirs in 1852, perhaps as an act of expiation, since during her life he had not quite known what to make of her. Hawthorne thought he did; thoroughly disliking her, he put her into his anti-

Brook Farm novel *The Blithedale Romance* as the imperious
Zenobia, who drowns.

Nathaniel Hawthorne figures in any brief discussion of
Transcendentalism for only two minor reasons. In almost
every way he was intellectually and temperamentally opposed
to Emerson, whom he once described in his *American Notebooks* (August 15, 1842) as "the mystic, stretching his hand
out of cloud-land, in vain search for something real; and the
man of sturdy sense, all whose ideas seem to be dug out of
his mind, hard and substantial, as he digs potatoes, beets,
carrots, and turnips, out of the earth. Mr. Emerson is a great
searcher for facts; but they seem to melt away, and become
unsubstantial in his grasp." In addition, Hawthorne satirized
Transcendentalism in "The Celestial Railroad" as "a German
by birth . . . as to his form, his features, his substance, and
his nature generally, it is the chief peculiarity of this huge
miscreant that neither he for himself, nor anybody for him,
has ever been able to describe them." Hawthorne adds that
when hastily seen the creature looks "somewhat like an ill-
proportioned figure, but considerably more like a heap of
fog and duskiness." But for two reasons Hawthorne almost
qualifies as a Transcendentalist: he did live for a few months
at Brook Farm, and in espousing in his fiction the theory that
sin sometimes causes a compensatory increase in knowledge
and sympathy he partly echoes Emerson's essay "Compensation." In most ways, however, Hawthorne was anti-Transcendental: he regarded unimproved nature as symbolic of
moral confusion, he did not greatly relish manual labor and
quickly tired of Brook Farm for this reason, he was rather
aloof from and suspicious of clamoringly conversational in-
tellectuals, he believed in the brotherhood of mankind only
as a brotherhood of sinners, he felt that self-reliance rather
than reliance upon tradition and social customs was a danger-

ous game, and he distrusted all reform that did not begin by reforming what in "Earth's Holocaust" he called "that foul cavern, the human heart."

Frederic Henry Hedge, the son of a Harvard logician, was a brilliant young student of German literature. Alone among Americans of his time, he read Immanuel Kant in the original. Retaining his interest in German philosophy, he urged it upon Margaret Fuller, J. F. Clarke, and George Ripley. Hedge became a Unitarian minister in New England and started teaching in the Harvard Divinity School in the late 1850's. He published the first article on Coleridge in America (in 1833). He officially founded the Transcendental Club, which for a short time he humorously dubbed the Hedge Club, by which title Emerson always referred to it. He popularized German literature, especially Goethe's *Faust,* and other foreign literature, by numerous writings of his own, which in addition included religious treatises. Hedge puzzled but ultimately intrigued and impressed Emerson.

Julia Ward Howe remained on the outskirts of Transcendentalism, having a mercurial, philanthropic husband in Dr. Samuel Gridley Howe and also having many literary irons in fires of her own. But her great interest in abolition and woman suffrage naturally led her to associate in varying degrees with Emerson, W. H. Channing, Theodore Parker, and other Transcendentalists. She wrote a life of Margaret Fuller. In her *Reminiscences,* Mrs. Howe seems to agree with those who, like Charles Dickens and C. P. Cranch, ridiculed the excesses of Transcendentalism; however, she also records her thorough sympathy both with its idealism, which stemmed from German works she was capable of reading and understanding, and with its enthusiastic spirit of general emancipation, which naturally carried into abolition.

Theodore Parker was a poverty-stricken and hard-handed

farm lad who by his own intellectual brilliance went ir-
regularly through Harvard and then its Divinity School to
become a linguist with twenty languages at his command, a
Unitarian minister, an effective and popular orator, and a
fiery would-be reformer of more abuses than simply slavery.
He broke with Unitarianism to become a controversial
Transcendentalist; at this time he defended Emerson and his
"Divinity School Address" from a weak and conservative
attack by Andrews Norton, recently retired from the Divinity
School but still its bland leader. Parker then became an
intermittent preacher in Boston, took a brief trip to Europe,
and returned to speak even more passionately for various
reforms. He advocated abolition of slavery by a touching
appeal to every individual to regenerate his own morality.
He knew Lincoln, who adapted a line from one of Parker's
speeches for the last sentence of the "Gettysburg Address."
When Parker knew that he was going to die prematurely,
of exhaustion and lung hemorrhages, he was every bit as
serene as Thoreau. He wrote a farewell sermon-letter to the
Congregational Society of Boston which had been supporting
him, and in his magnificent report he summed up the
Transcendental movement. He explained that he based his
beliefs on "certain great primal intuitions of human nature,
which depend on no logical process of demonstration, but are
rather facts of consciousness given by the instinctive action of
human nature itself." He then specified the three most important of these intuitions: an instinctive consciousness that
there is a God, an awareness that there is a moral law independent of ourselves which we ought to obey, and an intuition that the essential and individual part of oneself is
immortal. Parker went on poetically to praise Emerson for
helping him to find himself spiritually during his revolt
from Unitarianism: "The brilliant genius of Emerson rose

in the winter nights, and hung over Boston, drawing the eyes of ingenuous young people to look up to that great, new star, a beauty and a mystery, which charmed for the moment, while it gave also perennial inspiration, as it led them forward along new paths, and towards new hopes. America has seen no such sight before; it is not less a blessed wonder now." Shortly thereafter, Parker went on to Italy and died in 1860 at the age of fifty.

Elizabeth Peabody was the long-lived friend of dozens of Transcendentalists and other men of letters in the Boston area. She was the sister of Sophia Peabody, Hawthorne's wife, and of Mary Peabody, Horace Mann's wife. Elizabeth never married, but taught school for a while, part of the time theorizing Transcendentally with her colleague Alcott, became William Ellery Channing the elder's secretary, and invited Margaret Fuller to hold intellectual conversations in her Boston home. Then Miss Peabody opened a Salem bookshop, where many of the Transcendental Club meetings took place. She published the *Dial* magazine, edited by Miss Fuller and later by Emerson, and became friendly with Thoreau, whose far-reaching "Civil Disobedience" essay she first printed in a collection which she called *Aesthetic Papers*. Just before the Civil War she returned to matters educational, opening America's first kindergarten, founded on happiness, love, and faith. Later in life she became something of a little old institution, lending her dignified name to innumerable would-be reformers and possibly providing the model for Henry James's feminist Miss Birdseye in his novel *The Bostonians*.

George Ripley was a practical leader of the Transcendental movement. After graduating from Harvard and then its Divinity School, he began while still a minister to publish a Unitarian magazine which he called the *Christian Examiner* and which quickly became so liberal that Andrews Norton,

bland spokesman for official Unitarianism, lumped it and
Emerson together under the label of infidelity. Undaunted,
Ripley came to Emerson's defense after the latter's "Divinity
School Address," became one of the founding members of the
Transcendental Club, began with F. H. Hedge to edit the
massive *Specimens of Foreign Standard Literature* (which
provided some Continental philosophical support for the
thinking of the Club), and helped Margaret Fuller manage
the *Dial,* which he had helped to establish. After again an-
noying the Norton camp of Unitarians by additional liberal
writing, Ripley left the ministry and became president of
the Brook Farm organization. Living at Brook Farm for
several years, he edited its little magazine the *Harbinger,*
which in New York survived the depressing and costly col-
lapse of the communal farm. Ripley followed Margaret Fuller
as a literary critic on Horace Greeley's *Tribune* for several
decades. After his Catholic-convert wife's death, Ripley married
a German widow and took a couple of European tours. Emerson relied upon Ripley's business sense, such as it was,
and on his ability to push things through, and he greatly
appreciated the quiet heroism with which Ripley resigned
in 1841 from the Unitarian ministry because of conscience,
since Emerson had done the same thing nine years earlier
for substantially the same reasons if with somewhat more
fanfare.

Henry David Thoreau is really the only contemporary
of Emerson who bears comparison with him as a Transcendental man of letters. As an active Transcendentalist, he
was Emerson's superior. He was also closest to Emerson,
having been first noticed by him, frequently encouraged, sent
briefly to Emerson's brother William on Staten Island as tutor
for his children, and even hired as handyman around Emerson's house, installed there during Emerson's second trip

abroad (in 1847-1848), and finally eulogized movingly by Emerson upon his premature death in 1862. However, it is shallow to say, as is often said, that Thoreau merely practiced what Emerson preached. Thoreau was far more of a rugged individualist, earning his keep by efficient little bursts of varied homely labor, building his immortal shack with his own hands on Emerson's property beside Walden Pond, refusing to pay taxes in 1846 to a government condoning the extension of slave-land during the Mexican War, urging a most subversive form of civil disobedience and loathing those who acquired and revered property, worshiping nature far closer to mud and swamp than Emerson usually got, and maintaining complete serenity in the face of initial public indifference to his message. Thoreau's *Walden* is perhaps a better Transcendental document, artistically and substantively, than any one work by Emerson. And Thoreau's life and philosophy are completely harmonious with most of the tenets of the Transcendental movement: in nature Thoreau found material facts which flowered for him into Transcendental truths, was manually the handiest of literate handymen, truly lived in the spirit rather than in or on property, honored his body as the temporary material temple of the Lord and always modestly asserted that he and God were on friendly terms since he mystically partook of the Over-Soul, regarded a grove of calm beech trees as the only church in which he wanted to worship, and was such a living example of individualism that he wanted his readers not to follow him but to recognize instead that his sermon was simply that they should follow their own highest instincts—just as he did. Thoreau and Emerson were in agreement in opposing their Transcendental brethren for espousing intellectual companionships: they were equally ill at ease when surrounded or even approached by disciples, although Emerson was the more tactful of the two under such circumstances. In his eulogy, Emerson wrote as follows of Thoreau: " 'I love Henry,' said one of his friends, 'but I cannot like him; and as for taking his arm, I should as soon think of taking the arm of an elm tree.' " It is suspected that the friend making this comment was Emerson, who in his journals once recorded the following Thoreauvian comments: "Friends descend to meet" and "I like man, but not men." The biographical facts concerning Thoreau are briefly these. He was the only Concordian born in Concord, where he also died. He attended Harvard and early in his reading career went his eclectic way much as Emerson did. He never married. He sought as a profession simply being a lover of nature and a recorder of his thoughts. He lived for two years in a hut beside Walden Pond and celebrated in his book *Walden* that experiment of reducing life to its simplest terms. He kept a gigantic journal which came to 2,000,000 words over a twenty-four-year span. He wrote many other works, including *A Week on the Concord and Merrimack Rivers,* "Civil Disobedience," "Life Without Principle," *The Maine Woods, Cape Cod,* and many superb essays and poems and lectures, including a ringing defense of Captain John Brown.

Jones Very was a pathetic figure. His Salem sea-captain father took him on a trip to Russia once. He was an intelligent student at Harvard and tutored in Greek while studying at the Divinity School. But then he moved from Unitarianism to a semi-insane mysticism, under the spell of which he claimed to have religious and poetic visions. Early in his career Elizabeth Peabody sensed his worth and recommended him to Emerson, who characteristically pierced the young man's eccentricities and saw his genuine if muted genius. In 1838 he was committed for a short time to an asylum. One year later, Emerson supervised the publication of a book by

Very called *Essays and Poems*. J. F. Clarke was kind enough to publish many of Very's poems in the *Western Messenger* the same year. The Emerson of "Bacchus" was obliged to listen sympathetically when Very claimed divine inspiration for his poetry, which indeed is often exceedingly moving.

All of these Transcendentalists and more, of various shades of intensity, Emerson knew and aided in one way or another. Almost all of them looked up to him for intellectual guidance, spiritual refreshment, and practical help. His writings and personal counsel are reflected in their published work. Naturally they differed among themselves and sometimes with him, but all of them shared with him the same fervent belief in the basic tenets of Transcendentalism.

Beliefs

It is hard to summarize the many tenets of Transcendentalism, which come from Plato, Germany, the Orient, and America, and are espoused in partly harmonious but often contradictory and even conflicting forms by Emerson and his friends. However, in a single inadequate sentence one might say that Transcendentalism was an eclectic espousal of the over-riding values of individual feeling, intuition, conscience, and idealistic imagination; a consequent faith in the potentialities of the common man, in democracy, in nature, and in a gentle, fraternal, pervasive God; and a concomitant indifference to high society, cold science, and systematic institutions like schools and churches.

Probably the most important Transcendental value was the belief in the supremacy of intuition over induction, imagination over logic, and the conscience over any form of traditional authority. Emerson regarded intuition as "angel-whispering,—which discomfits the conclusions of nations and of years!" ("Experience"). Intuition is the sudden flash of inspiration, which permits the responsible, imaginative mind—in conjunction with the heart—to see into the workings of all reality in ways which the plodding scholar, with only his limited understanding to aid him, could never do. Faith in the rightness of one's own gleams of the truth and therefore in the rightness of one's own conscience gives a new dignity to the individual. Hence Emerson can adjure us to study ourselves. For, as he says, "the ancient precept, 'Know thyself,' and the modern precept, 'Study nature,' became at last one maxim" ("Nature"). This statement in itself, like many others in the intuitively brilliant essay "Nature," is a flashing intuition. And the companion-pieces of "Nature," that is, "The American Scholar" and "Divinity School Address," also reveal Emerson's faith in the individual's own intuitions and Emerson's consequent indifference and even animosity toward institutionalized learning and worship.

Another important belief of the Transcendentalists was in the real or potential worth of the common man. If an ordinary individual's insights could lead him to profounder truths concerning God than school and church could teach him, then surely his right to regard himself as the political and social equal to the highest and mightiest should not be questioned. Early in his career, Emerson embraced "the common," explored and sat "at the feet of the familiar, the low," and happily greeted as a "sign of our times, also marked by an analogous political movement, . . . the new importance given to the single person" ("The American Scholar"). Every man is of transcendent value because each of us shares in the Over-Soul, is therefore perfectable and even divine. This is the point of the essay "The Over-Soul," and in his essay "Plato," Emerson approvingly quotes from a Hindu text as follows: "What is the great end of all, you shall now learn from me. It is soul,—one in all bodies . . ." It ought to follow, given this brotherhood of equally invaluable souls, that thorough-going democracy—Jacksonian rather than merely Jeffersonian—would be Emerson's ideal political system. However, democrat though he was in theory, Emerson in real life was often fastidious, was rarely rough and ready, and believed that while all men could avail themselves of divine inspiration through the Over-Soul, it happened that only a few did so in any one epoch. These representative men—representative of everyone's best potentialities—naturally guided the rest, the rude mob, of whom Emerson once wrote in this unflattering fashion: "Masses are rude, lame, unmade, pernicious in their demands and influence, and need not to be flattered but to be schooled. . . . Masses! the calamity is the masses" ("Considerations by the Way," in *The Conduct of Life*). This is extreme, and Emerson, knowing it, tempered his harsh judgment by often suggesting that each unwashed member of the masses was potentially, if not actually, a doer or a poet open to all the influences of God and nature. As he says in "Nature," "A man is a god in ruins. . . . Infancy is the perpetual Messiah, which comes into the arms of fallen men, and pleads with them to return to paradise."

Obviously nature, like one's intuitions and his fellow men, was also an object of faith for the Transcendentalists. The values of nature are many: it is mysterious and poetic, and it shows man the secrets of beauty and harmony. At times nature seems a tissue of symbols, a glowing embodiment of the mind of God, lavishly pouring out images and messages for our sake. At other times its incredible complexity tempts us to think that it exists only as a reflection of man's ranging imagination and spirit. Emerson has the typical romantic's love of nature, like William Wordsworth and William Cullen Bryant rather than Lord Byron. Emerson preferred rural to urban locales, returned to the common soil for refreshment after the fray—"before the vote is taken, dig away in your garden" ("Experience")—found in natural growth and change evidence to support his theory of organic art, and fancied that scientific discoveries concerning natural phenomena would lead the way to philosophical discoveries. He wrote in his journal that "The Religion that is afraid of science dishonors God and commits suicide." And he wrote in his essay "Circles," "Does the fact look crass and material, threatening to degrade thy theory of spirit? Resist it not; it goes to refine and raise thy theory of matter just as much." Yet Emerson inevitably was at odds with the scientific method, since he relied on personal intuition rather than the cumulative efforts of groups of patient scientists. He read widely if non-professionally in contemporary scientific journals, but he did so like a poet and took from such reading only what happened to suit his unscientific intellectual endeavors of the moment.

This faith in self, the common man, and nature led the Transcendentalists to several idealistic conclusions. The most important among them are that goodness is everywhere and inevitable, that law for man should be regarded as more vital than law for thing, and that a fundamental unity underlies all apparent diversity.

Emerson has been wrongly accused of believing, like Pollyanna, that goodness automatically will defeat evil, indeed that evil is nothing but wrongly directed good. Out of context, the following statements support those who would so accuse their author: ". . . evil is good in the making . . ." ("Fate"), and "I could never give much reality to evil and pain" (*Journals*, June, 1861). But it is clearly enough shown in such dark essays of his as "Experience," "Montaigne," and

"Fate," and in several poems, that Emerson was well aware of the pervasiveness of evil and of its powerfully blighting effects. He wrote that "Every calamity is a spur" ("Fate"), which ought to suggest that he knew the reality of calamities but further that only after a real struggle with the devil does the good man know his strength, that only after sorrow does the optimist have the right to reveal his ultimate serenity.

In his "Channing Ode" Emerson wrote the following:

> There are two laws discrete,
> Not reconciled,
> Law for man, and law for thing;
> The last builds town and fleet,
> But it runs wild,
> And doth the man unking.

These lines are very important. They show Emerson's patent dualism and imply his search for monism; further, they indicate his awareness of the material advances of his country but with it his clear preference for human over property rights. The fact that "law for thing" too often obliterated "Law for man" depressed Emerson, particularly when he wrote the lines just quoted, late in the 1840's when the Mexican War seemed to him to augur the coming of Civil War. He sought philosophically to reconcile Deistic law for thing and Romantic law for man; in fact, he regarded that search to harmonize the inner nature of man and the outer nature of God as the fundamental intellectual challenge of man. Living as he did in an age of violent material expansion into the West, he clearly saw both the tangible successes of his adventurous countrymen, who were building "town and fleet," and the danger: those bent on simply amassing material wealth were indeed "unking[ing]" themselves, were abrogating their thrones and becoming "wild" beasts. In short, Emerson felt that men should hold human rights above material rights; those who do not are less men than things worshipping things. Shrewd Yankee though he was, Emerson all through his life held religious and intellectual and aesthetic values far above property rights. Most of the Transcendentalists did the same, especially Thoreau, of whom Emerson approvingly wrote: "He had no talent for wealth, and knew how to be poor without the least hint of squalor or inelegance" ("Thoreau"). Thoreau was more extreme than Emerson, who, however, might in those lines have been writing of himself, especially when he was young.

Inner and outer nature might be various and hard at times to harmonize, but Emerson sensed and often described the simple basic unity pervading all creation. Early in his career he considered "why all thought of multitude is lost in a tranquil sense of unity" ("Nature"). Later, discussing Knower, Doer, and Sayer, he added that "each of these three has the power of the others latent in him and his own, patent" ("The Poet"). Unity underlying variety is the theme of such poems, among many others, as "The Sphinx" (all things are "By one music enchanted") and "Brahma" ("Shadow and sunlight are the same"). To Emerson, nature created everything out of one material: "Compound it how she will, star, sand, fire, water, tree, man, it is still one stuff, and betrays the same properties" ("Nature," in *Essays, Second Series*). More than that, all matter which becomes living is quickened by the same vital force: "In all animal and vegetable forms, the physiologist concedes that no chemistry, no mechanics, can account for the facts, but a mysterious principle of life must be assumed, which not only inhabits the organ but makes the organ" ("The Method of Nature," an 1841 lecture). So, just as all men are linked through participation in the same Over-Soul, all living forms can be explained only by citing the identical enigma—the "mysterious principle of life," which is one and the same throughout the universe. Mystic as he was, Emerson often used outer nature merely as an inspiration, then closed his sensory organs to it and ecstatically let his soul become enveloped in beauty and truth. In such a mood he could conjure up expressions like the following: ". . . matter is a phenomenon, not a substance. . . . the world is a divine dream, from which we may presently awake to the glories and certainties of day" ("Nature"). And later: "We live by our imaginations, by our admirations, by our sentiments. The child walks amid heaps of illusions, which he does not like to have disturbed. . . . The man lives to other objects, but who dare affirm that they are more real?" ("Illusions"). What remained most real to Emerson was always the mystical experience. Less real to him was objective reality and what the understanding did with it all; more real, in fact the only ultimate reality, was what the imagination found when its user turned away from mere matter, oblivious to it: "there are the gods still sitting around him on their thrones,—they alone with him alone" ("Illusions").

Emerson was as well aware of variety as he was of unity. He writes in "Plato": "Two cardinal facts lie forever at the base; the one, and the two.—1. Unity, or Identity; and, 2. Variety. We unite all things by perceiving the law which pervades them; by perceiving the superficial differences and the profound resemblances. But every mental act,—this very perception of identity and oneness, recognizes the differences of things. Oneness and otherness. It is impossible to speak or to think without embracing both." But the main direction of his ever-tacking thought was toward unity which embraced variety. "Each and All" so ends: "I yielded myself to the perfect whole." "Initial, Dæmonic, and Celestial Love" moves up the ladder of love from Venus and Cupid, through beauty and grace, to heaven; in that poem Emerson writes of love, "the holy essence," as "One through separated souls." Similarly, all the varieties of life are unified too: in the epigraph to the essay "Nature" we read that

> . . . striving to be man, the worm
> Mounts through all the spires of form.

And the whole purpose of "Circles," Emerson's rarely printed but important essay, is to show that as the thinker spirals through his "fluid and volatile" universe of ideas, he constantly closes a comprehensive circle upon an intellectual unit: "Each new step we take in thought reconciles twenty seemingly discordant facts, as expressions of one law." As "Uriel" has it:

> Line in nature is not found;
> Unit and universe are round . . .

Perhaps the most bracing, the most comforting conclusion we can draw from all of Emerson stems from the implications of his deliberations on variety and unity. He urges us to try, as he did, to harmonize the splintering diversities we see all about us, and to believe that we and nature are interdependent, that one soul animates the whole world, and that man ascending "the spires of form" reaches and is the divine.

Effects

Both the immediate and the long-range consequences of the Transcendental movement and Emerson's central part in it were many. In the first place, the Transcendental Club was

established in 1836, the *Dial* magazine founded in 1840, and
the Brook Farm experiment begun in 1841. And in the second
place, effects both good and less than good were visible in
the decades of Emerson's decline and shortly after his death,
and are to a lesser extent apparent today. American Romantic
idealism owes much to Emerson, more to him in fact than to
any other single writer. Also American pragmatism finds
philosophical sanction in many of his utterances. He was a
source of inspiration for such diverse writers as Emily Dickinson, William James, John Jay Chapman, John Dewey, Robert
Frost, and Hart Crane, among many others. Adversely, pop-
lar interpretations of Emerson's theories concerning self-reliance, anti-materialism, and optimism often provided the
wrong kind of rationalization for Western expansion in particular and American acquisitiveness generally, while the
alleged shallowness of Emerson's remarks against logic and
against materialism helped to prepare America badly to face
some of the global horrors of the present century.

Back on the positive side, Emerson from almost the first
was a vital force in popularizing American thought and
writing abroad, especially in England, France, Germany, and
the Far East. Even more important, he is a continuingly
provocative and challenging thinker, who does for every age
what the great writers of the world always do—he poses old
questions which perennially need new answers, responses specifically fitted to the ever-changing times. He may have
written that "Each age . . . must write its own books; or
rather, each generation for the next succeeding" ("The American Scholar"). However, his works are for all times because
they address themselves to timeless problems—to the nature
of man, his relations to the world of people and things about
him, beauty and goodness and truth, freedom and fate, poetry,
time, and the soul and God.

Emerson pondered all of these subjects, in many of their ramifications. Since he was thoroughly human, his thought and modes of expression changed over the decades. But this fact only makes him the more undated, the more relevant to any given age. We can go to him with our problems and find, if not answers to them all, at least encouragement to continue the search. To all times Emerson's advice and example point in the healthy direction of individualism, courageous conduct, and ultimate justice.

VII. FOR FURTHER READING

Books and especially articles about Emerson are bewilderingly numerous. The following are suggested as being particularly illuminating.

Adams, Richard P. "Emerson and the Organic Metaphor," *PMLA,* LXIX (March, 1954), 117-130. Criticizes Emerson's interpretation of the universe as organic.

Atkinson, Brooks, ed. *The Complete Essays and Other Writings of Ralph Waldo Emerson.* The Modern Library. New York: Random House, 1940. Generous selections.

Berry, Edmund G. *Emerson's Plutarch.* Cambridge, Massachusetts: Harvard University Press, 1961. Specialized study of Emerson's acquaintance with Plutarch's writings and of Emerson's literary use of Plutarch's comments on simplicity, heroism, and stoicism.

Blair, Walter, and Clarence Faust. "Emerson's Literary Method," *Modern Philology,* XLII (November, 1944), 79-95. Suggests that Plato's twice-bisected line helps to explain Emerson's method of organizing his material, demonstrably in "Art," "The Poet," "Each and All," and "Threnody."

Brown, Stuart G. "Emerson's Platonism," *New England Quarterly,* XVIII (September, 1945), 325-345. Criticizes Emerson's inconsistencies, suggesting that they are due to his use of Platonism to support his experiential writing.

Cabot, James Elliot. *A Memoir of Ralph Waldo Emerson.* 2 vols. Boston and New York: Houghton Mifflin Company, 1887. Indispensable source of material by Emerson's friend and literary executor.

Cameron, Kenneth W. *Emerson the Essayist*. 2 vols. Raleigh, North Carolina: Thistle Press, 1945. Exhaustive material on Emerson's development through 1836, with stress upon his attitude toward nature.

Cameron, Kenneth Walter. *An Emerson Index: or, Names, Exempla, Sententiae, Symbols, Words, and Motifs in Selected Notebooks of Ralph Waldo Emerson*. Hartford, Connecticut: Transcendental Books, 1958. Highly useful in many ways to specialists.

Campbell, Harry Modean. "Emerson and Whitehead," *PMLA*, LXXV (December, 1960), 577-582. Competent specialized study which demonstrates Emerson's relevance to modern thought.

Carpenter, Frederic Ives. *Emerson and Asia*. Cambridge, Massachusetts: Harvard University Press, 1930. Significant study of Emerson's indebtedness to Oriental (especially Indian) philosophy, religion, and literature.

Carpenter, Frederic Ives. *Emerson Handbook*. New York: Hendricks House, Inc., 1953. Excellent handbook, in four parts: Emerson's biography, Emerson's prose and poetry, Emerson's ideas, and Emerson and world literature; with admirably thorough bibliographies.

Carpenter, Frederic I., ed. *Ralph Waldo Emerson: Representative Selections*. New York: American Book Company, 1934. Excellent early edition, with useful introduction and notes.

Chapman, John Jay. "Emerson" (from *Emerson and Other Essays, 1898*), in *The Selected Writings of John Jay Chapman*. Garden City, New York: Doubleday & Company, 1959. The finest late nineteenth-century general estimate of Emerson.

Christy, Arthur. *The Orient in American Transcendentalism: A Study of Emerson, Thoreau, and Alcott*. New York: Columbia University Press, 1932. The definitive study of the subject.

Cook, Reginald L., ed. *Ralph Waldo Emerson: Selected Prose and Poetry*. Rinehart Editions. New York: Holt, Rinehart, & Winston, 1950. A well-balanced selection.

Emerson, Edward Waldo, and Waldo Emerson Forbes, eds. *The Journals of Ralph Waldo Emerson*. 10 vols. Cambridge, Massachusetts: Printed at the Riverside Press, 1909-1914. Long a standard, this edition is being superseded by that of William H. Gilman and his associates, 1960 on.

Gilman, William H., *et al.*, eds. *The Journals and Miscellaneous Notebooks of Ralph Waldo Emerson*. Cambridge, Massachusetts: Harvard University Press, 1960 on. This definitive edition of Emerson's journals and notebooks, now in progress and ultimately to total sixteen volumes or so, will supersede that of Edward Waldo Emerson and Waldo Emerson Forbes, 1909-1914.

Gohdes, Clarence, ed. *Uncollected Lectures by Ralph Waldo Emerson*. New York: William Edwin Rudge, 1932. Reprints six lectures by Emerson on "American Life," 1864-1865, and one lecture on "Natural Religion," 1869.

Gray, Henry David. *Emerson: A Statement of New England Transcendentalism as Expressed in the Philosophy of Its Chief Exponent*. Stanford, California: Stanford University Press, 1917. Reprinted by New York: Frederick Ungar Publishing Co., 1958. Admirably thorough and formal presentation of Emerson's poetic and religious philosophy of permanence, correspondence, evolutionary progress, reform, beauty, and morality.

Hopkins, Vivian C. *Spires of Form: A Study of Emerson's Aesthetic Theory*. Cambridge, Massachusetts: Harvard University Press, 1951. Study of Emerson's theory of organic art as applied to literature and other arts.

Horton, Rod W., and Herbert W. Edwards. *Backgrounds of American Literary Thought*. New York: Appleton-Century-Crofts, Inc., 1952. Contains the best brief account of Unitarianism and Transcendentalism readily available.

Konvitz, Milton R., and Stephen E. Whicher, eds. *Emerson: A Collection of Critical Essays*. Englewood Cliffs, New Jersey: Prentice-Hall, Inc., 1962. Fifteen essays by perceptive critics and admirers of Emerson, including William James, John Dewey, George Santayana, Robert Frost, and Newton Arvin.

Kronman, Jeanne. "Three Unpublished Lectures of Ralph Waldo Emerson," *New England Quarterly*, XIX (March, 1946), 98-110. Three lectures not in McGiffert (which see).

Kuntz, Joseph M. *Poetry Explication: A Checklist of Interpretations since 1925 of British and American Poems Past and Present*. Denver: Alan Swallow, rev. ed., 1962. Bibliographical citations of explications of several Emerson poems.

Linscott, Robert N., ed. *The Journals of Ralph Waldo Emerson*. The Modern Library. New York: Random House, 1960. An excellent recent abridgment.

Matthiessen, F. O. *The American Renaissance: Art and Expression in the Age of Emerson and Whitman*. New York: Oxford University Press, 1941. Analyzes Emerson's life and works, and sets both in the context of the careers of Thoreau, Hawthorne, Melville, and Whitman; illuminating insights into Emerson's aesthetics.

McCormick, John O. "Emerson's Theory of Human Greatness," *New England Quarterly*, XXVI (September, 1953), 291-314. Considers Emerson's optimistic faith in mankind but distrust of the masses.

McGiffert, Arthur Cushman, Jr., ed. *Young Emerson Speaks: Unpublished Discourses on Many Subjects.* Boston: Houghton Mifflin Company, 1938. Twenty-five of Emerson's most important sermons (excluding "The Lord's Supper" and "Right Hand of Fellowship," often previously printed); includes an excellent introduction, notes, a list of all of Emerson's sermons, and index.

Miller, Perry, ed. *The American Transcendentalists: Their Prose and Poetry.* Garden City, New York: Doubleday Anchor Books, 1957. Inexpensive anthology of Transendental writings on nature, religion, art, politics, and society; with helpful notes and brief bibliography. This collection deliberately omits the best of Emerson and Thoreau, since they are readily available elsewhere.

Miller, Perry, ed. *The Transcendentalists: An Anthology.* Cambridge, Massachusetts: Harvard University Press, 1950. Anthology of more than a hundred significant selections or parts thereof, often theological, by all of the important Transcendentalists, with helpful notes and bibliography. Emerson and Thoreau are deliberately slighted since their works are readily available elsewhere.

Nicoloff, Philip L. *Emerson on Race and History: An Examination of English Traits.* New York: Columbia University Press, 1961. Dissertation on Emerson's book *English Traits* and the part it played in the evolution of Emerson's concept of race and history.

Paris, Bernard J. "Emerson's 'Bacchus,'" *Modern Language Quarterly,* XXIII (June, 1962), 150-159. A cogent analysis of the structure and development of "Bacchus."

Paul, Sherman. *Emerson's Angle of Vision: Man and Nature in American Experience.* Cambridge, Massachusetts: Harvard University Press, 1952. An intricate study of Emerson's idea of the correspondence between material and nonmaterial reality and of his dialectical approach to problems stemming from the doctrine of correspondence.

Perry, Bliss. *Emerson Today*. Princeton, New Jersey: Princeton University Press, 1931. Sympathetic, charming, readable treatment of Emerson's personal and intellectual life.

Perry, Bliss, ed. *The Heart of Emerson's Journals*. Boston and New York: Houghton Mifflin Company, 1926. Reprinted by New York: Dover Publications, Inc., 1958. A careful abridgment.

Pollock, Robert C. "Ralph Waldo Emerson: The Single Vision," in *American Classics Reconsidered: A Christian Appraisal,* ed. Harold C. Gardiner. New York: Charles Scribner's Sons, 1958. An excellent comprehensive essay.

Rusk, Ralph L., ed. *The Letters of Ralph Waldo Emerson*. 6 vols. New York: Columbia University Press, 1939. A definitive presentation of all the letters not previously published, with a calendar of all other letters; with an excellent introduction, notes, and index.

Rusk, Ralph L. *The Life of Ralph Waldo Emerson*. New York: Charles Scribner's Sons, 1949. The definitive scholarly biography.

Schneider, Herbert W. "The Transcendental Temper," in *A History of American Philosophy*. New York: Columbia University Press, 1946. Hard-headed criticism of the philosophy of Transcendentalism in the context of American philosophy in general; has many suggestions for further reading.

Scudder, Townsend. *The Lonely Wayfaring Man: Emerson and Some Englishmen*. London and New York: Oxford University Press, 1936. A detailed portrait of Emerson in the company of many British contemporaries, notably Thomas Carlyle.

Slater, Joseph, ed. *The Correspondence of Emerson and Carlyle*. New York: Columbia University Press, 1964. The definitive edition of this vitally important correspondence, with an excellent introduction, notes, and index.

Spiller, Robert E. "Ralph Waldo Emerson," in *Literary History of the United States,* ed. Robert E. Spiller *et al.* New York: The Macmillan Company, 1948, rev. ed. 1963. A splendidly balanced essay on Emerson, the man and the writer. Useful parts of this literary history also are the *Bibliography,* 1948, and *Bibliographical Supplement,* ed. Richard M. Ludwig, 1959; these bibliographies were reissued in a combined edition in 1963.

Stovall, Floyd. "Emerson," in *Eight American Authors: A Review of Research and Criticism,* ed. Floyd Stovall. New York: The Modern Language Association of America, 1956. With *Bibliographical Supplement* by J. Chesley Mathews. New York: W. W. Norton & Company, 1963. The best selective and descriptive bibliography of Emerson. The serious student should also consult the annual bibliography of the *Publications of the Modern Language Association,* the annual bibliography of the *Explicator,* and the quarterly bibliography of *American Literature,* for an indication of current scholarship on Emerson.

Strauch, Carl F. "The Year of Emerson's Poetic Maturity: 1834," *Philological Quarterly,* XXXIV (October, 1955), 353-377. An astute discussion of "The Rhodora," "Xenophon," "Each and all," and "The Snow-Storm."

Thrall, William Flint, and Addison Hibbard. *A Handbook to Literature.* New York: The Odyssey Press, 1936; rev. ed. by C. Hugh Holman, 1960. Lucid and helpful definitions of all critical and related terms, an understanding of which is necessary for an appreciation of Emerson as well as other writers.

Tucker, Ellen Louisa. *One First Love: The Letters of Ellen Louisa Tucker to Ralph Waldo Emerson,* ed. Edith W.

Gregg. Cambridge, Massachusetts: Harvard University Press, 1962. An aid in understanding Emerson's relationship to Ellen Tucker, who later became his first wife; his letters to her have evidently been lost.

Van Doren, Mark, ed. *The Portable Emerson*. The Viking Portable Library. New York: The Viking Press, 1946. Wide and generous selections.

Whicher, George F., ed. *The Transcendental Revolt Against Materialism*. No. 4 in Problems in American Civilization. Boston: D. C. Heath and Company, 1949. Nine important items by various persons, including Emerson and a few of his contemporaries, with a valuable introduction and bibliographical suggestions.

Whicher, Stephen E., and Robert E. Spiller, eds. *The Early Lectures of Ralph Waldo Emerson*. Cambridge, Massachusetts: Harvard University Press, 1959 on. This excellently edited collection of Emerson's early lectures (1833-1847) will eventually comprise three volumes or so.

Whicher, Stephen E. *Freedom and Fate: An Inner Life of Ralph Waldo Emerson*. Philadelphia: University of Pennsylvania Press, 1953. A superb treatment of Emerson's dialectical development: self-reliance and then skepticism leading to a synthesis in humanistic balance and acceptance.

Whicher, Stephen E., ed. *Selections from Ralph Waldo Emerson: An Organic Anthology*. Riverside Editions. Boston: Houghton Mifflin Company, 1957. An elaborately and provocatively edited selection of thirteen prose works and much poetry.

Whitaker, Thomas R. "The Riddle of Emerson's 'Sphinx,' " *American Literature,* XXVII (May, 1955), 179-195. A provocative reading of "The Sphinx."

Yohannan, J. D. "The Influence of Persian Poetry upon Emerson's Work," *American Literature,* XV (March, 1943), 25-

41. An expert demonstration of the influence of Hafiz and Saadi on "Bacchus," "To J. W.," "Give All to Love," "Mithridates," "Terminus," and other poems by Emerson.

Young, Charles Lowell. *Emerson's Montaigne.* New York: The Macmillan Company, 1941. A specialized study of Emerson's response to Montaigne as a man, writer, skeptic, and moralist.